ABOUT SPONTANEOUS COMBUSTION

Sherry Kramer

BROADWAY PLAY PUBLISHING INC
New York
www.broadwayplaypublishing.com
info@broadwayplaypublishing.com

First printing: September 2010
I S B N: 978-0-88145-384-6

Book design: Marie Donovan
Word processing: Microsoft Word
Typographic controls: Ventura Publisher
Typeface: Palatino
Printed and bound in the U S A

ABOUT THE AUTHOR

Sherry Kramer is the recipient of an N E A, a New York Foundation for the Arts Fellowship, a McKnight National Fellowship, and a commission from the Audrey Skirball-Kenis Theater Project. Her plays have been produced here and abroad and include productions at Actors Theater of Louisville Humana Festival, Yale Repertory Theater, The Second Stage, Woolly Mammoth Theater, Soho Repertory Theater, Ensemble Studio Theater, Annex Theater, InterAct Theater, and the Theater of the First Amendment. She was the first national member of New Dramatists. Other plays include: WHEN SOMETHING WONDERFUL ENDS, DAVID'S REDHAIRED DEATH (The Jane Chambers Award), THE WALL OF WATER (L A Women in Theater Award), WHAT A MAN WEIGHS (Weissberger Playwriting Award, New York Drama League Award, The Marvin Taylor Playwriting Award), A THING OF BEAUTY, THE BAY OF FUNDY: AN ADAPTATION OF ONE LINE FROM THE MAYOR OF CASTERBRIDGE, THINGS THAT BREAK, THE WORLD AT ABSOLUTE ZERO, THE MAD MASTER, THE LONG ARMS OF JUPITER (a croquet performance piece), PARTIAL OBJECTS, THE LAW MAKES EVENING FALL, THE MIDDLE OF THE DAY, A PERMANENT SIGNAL, THE RULING PASSION, THE RELEASE OF A LIVE PERFORMANCE, THE MASTER AND MARGARITA (a singing-theater adaptation), NANO AND NICKI IN BOCA RATON, NAPOLEON'S CHINA (a play with music), IVANHOE, ARK., and THE RULING PASSION. She holds M F As from the Iowa Writers' Workshop (Fiction) and the Iowa Playwrights' Workshop, and teaches playwriting at Bennington College, The Michener Center for Writers at the University of Texas, Austin, and the Iowa Playwrights' Workshop, where she was previously head of the workshop.

CHARACTERS & SETTING

AMALIA, *unmarried, unemployed twenty-five year old*
ROB, *ex-Assistant D A, late twenties*
VICTORIA, AMALIA's *mother*
GLEN, AMALIA's *father*
AUNT EMILY, GLEN's *maiden aunt, over eighty*
MARY CATHERINE, AMALIA's *older sister, early thirties*

AMALIA's *bedroom is downstage, off center to the right. The kitchen is elongated, fish-lensed up stage around the bedroom, and is visible through the suggested walls of the bedroom.*

The backdoor is downstage left, feeding off from that edge of the kitchen, and opens onto steps and a small patio.

Wedged in-between the stage right side of AMALIA's *room and the kitchen is a good sized bathroom, opening into the bedroom.*

Following the outer perimeter of the kitchen, slightly elevated, is a hallway, containing a string of closets: linen closets, clothes closets, and a sporting goods closet.

ACT ONE: Morning
ACT TWO: The next day

ACT ONE

(*Lights on in* AMALIA's *room. Her bed is made, and on the floor is a pile of thirty to forty pieces of her clothing. The door to the walk-in closet is open, and the light is on.*)

(AUNT EMILY *hurries along the upper hallway carrying a stack of laundry. She enters the kitchen and loads the washing machine.*)

(GLEN, *wearing his bathrobe and slippers, switches on the light and steps out on the back porch. He holds his hand out, checking for rain.*)

(VICTORIA *switches on the kitchen light and places a small grocery bag on the kitchen counter.*)

(AMALIA *steps out of her closet, holding a handful of clothing. She throws it on the pile.*)

AMALIA: Of course, I'm not going to burst into flames right before your very eyes. (*She looks down at the sweater she's wearing and struggles to take it off and throw it on the pile.*) Still, there is the possibility. (*She selects another sweater from an open drawer, hesitates, throws it on the pile and puts another one on.*) It's the possibility.

VICTORIA: I'm not saying it had to be the biggest, they were three for a dollar, well they say that the odds are always stacked against you so the house wins no matter what your system. No, I didn't mind if my three for a dollar did not represent for me, the most per penny...not that I wouldn't have minded winning that extra bite, that additional slice, that ounce or two, that...victory. For my family. That very small, it is always very small—victory.

GLEN: (*He sticks a wet finger in the air to test the breeze, and uncovers a massive panel of weather instruments.*) This won't hurt a bit, never does, does it, I know, I know that by now.

VICTORIA: Of course there is that sense of pride, other women sneaking looks into your shopping cart. There have been times in my life when their jealousy...other women's jealousy...has been enough for me. But this morning, at the supermarket... (*She falters, then regains her composure.*) I did not care that it be without a bruise, or a cut, or a soft place that would become a bruise, in secret, in the bag in the trunk on the way home. I didn't care.

(AUNT EMILY *continues sorting laundry, giving no sign that she is listening.*)

VICTORIA: All I wanted...all I wanted... (*She pulls a medium sized cantaloupe out of the bag.*) Well, all right, you say, so you develop a keen eye, a sense of touch and smell, you adapt, you prepare yourself for that relationship you must have with a piece of fruit...a piece of fruit...you get yourself what you need. And you walk into that supermarket and you present yourself to the rows and stacks and refrigerated cases, graded and inspected and so, so easily yours...

AUNT EMILY: What did you get?

VICTORIA: A cantaloupe. I picked out this cantaloupe, and I was sure...reasonably sure...that this cantaloupe would be...that it would be...and so I was reaching for the next, the second cantaloupe, reaching the same way, I knew, I would reach for the third, reaching to touch and smell and feel and shake when...when...

AUNT EMILY: (*Hefting the cantaloupe*) Nice lookin' melon. Not a Rocky Ford, though, your Rocky Fords come later in the season, you wait and you wait for them and one day there's a whole bin of 'em and the next there's none. That way with your Temples too, and your Bings. (*Poking her head in the refrigerator*) You get anymore or just the one?

VICTORIA: This one.

AUNT EMILY: Just the one?

VICTORIA: I'm telling you...I reached out my hand but I couldn't tell. All of them stacked up there but who could really tell? I pulled back my hand and I said, I said out loud, *"I have lost the will to live here in the produce department."* (*She starts to cry.*)

AUNT EMILY: You said it out loud?

VICTORIA: I lost the will to live in the produce department at Safeway and I said it out loud.

AUNT EMILY: No one answered you.

VICTORIA: No.

AUNT EMILY: Well they shouldn't have heard you either. Of course, whether they did or not or whose fault it would be is six of one half dozen of the other.

(VICTORIA *sobs louder.*)

AUNT EMILY: Now you stop that crying. Glen shouldn't see you crying, you crying like this. He shouldn't, he knows better, but if you don't stop crying then he will.

AMALIA: (*Holding a dress up in front of her*) One hundred percent rayon. Believe me, nothing burns as fast as some of these synthetics. Just because there's been no official government testing on the fire retardent qualities of garments during spontaneous combustion is no reason why, as consumers, we shouldn't all be more aware. (*She throws the dress onto the pile.*) The fire starts internally. Inside, all at once.

GLEN: (*Reading dials and making notations. He speaks in a buddy-buddy, man to man tone of voice.*) Used to make me mad as hell, to wake up and come outside of a morning to a clear blue sky that was sure to cloud up into soup by noon. Felt like there was some kind of promise broken. Expecting, assuming—you know what assuming makes? The word? It makes an ass of "U" and me. (*Laughs at his own joke*) Well, but it's the weather that makes asses of men and not the other way around. Always assuming some kind of correlation between that moment you look out your bedroom window and the weather...my god, you look at all the items you've got to consider determine the exact moment that you'll wedge your fat up on one elbow and you'll make the effort to focus out the window you promised your wife you'd wash last weekend so you can decide—declare—believe what kind of day it's gonna be from that one instant of weather?

Or to put it all more simply: the weather does not get up in the morning when you do, sir, and since you cannot be on hand constantly to watch, to test, to monitor, to decide—this baby— (*He proudly touches the weather panel.*) —this baby does it for you. We have a complete line of household models... (*He snaps out of his salespitch.*) But none as complete or as househeld as this. Built the whole damn house around it. (*He shines up a dial with his robe.*)

AMALIA: All this would be a meaningless precaution, if it were a precaution. But it's more than that. It's an understanding. Between me and what's inside me. An understanding that feels like the moment when one of a pair of Siamese Twins, sharing the same body from the waist down, manually discovers masturbation.

ROB: (*Poking his head out from under the pile of clothes*) You mean it feels like it feels to the other twin?

AMALIA: Yes.

ROB: Then this understanding of yours must feel real good.

AMALIA: You know that's not what I mean. (*She flings a dress in his face.*)

(GLEN *enters the kitchen.* AUNT EMILY *returns to her washing machine.*)

VICTORIA: Well? How's the weather?

GLEN: Thirty-five years we've been married, thirty-five years, the thirty-five just previous to this one, and you can ask me that question?

VICTORIA: I just meant for golf, Glen, the weather for golf, that's all I meant—

GLEN: It looks fine out there, Vickie, I know my business, a man retires, his business doesn't stop being his business.

VICTORIA: Then you'll be leaving for the course right away?

GLEN: Vickie, darling, I said the weather was fine. Which is to say, as I have always said: Bad weather is better than no weather at all.

VICTORIA: Then—it's not fine?

GLEN: (*Softly, so* VICTORIA *can't hear*) I've seen a day like this before.

ROB: Not that one! Come on, please, not that one too.

AMALIA: This one?

ROB: It's my favorite.

AMALIA: This old rag?

ROB: You look...you look so special in it.

AMALIA: Special?

ROB: Very special.

AMALIA: (*Drops it on the pile like a hot potato*) That settles it. It's the most dangerous of them all and it has to go.

ROB: Couldn't you—couldn't you put it on one last time? Just so I could see you in it?

AMALIA: I certainly could not. It's not safe.

ROB: You wouldn't have to wear it for long...just for a minute or two.

(AMALIA *shakes her head, no.* ROB *picks up the dress.*)

AMALIA: Oh, I know what you're thinking, buster, you're thinking you can maybe talk me into wearing it a little, then a little more, well you can't. Put it back. I said *I know what you're thinking!*

(ROB *drops the dress.*)

VICTORIA: I'll start breakfast, then. I'll just open up this cantaloupe, cut it open, and then we'll see—then we'll know what's inside it.

AUNT EMILY: Don't go cutting any for me. It's a good looking melon, there's no saying it isn't, but isn't cantaloupe the thing that fat people are always eating to lose weight? A curious way to lose weight, always eating things, they should stop eating altogether, it's eating that's gotten them into trouble in the first place. It's a good looking melon but it reminds me of fat people who want to be thin people, it's what they're always eating, after all.

GLEN: You mean after all the trouble Victoria took shopping for that cantaloupe—

AUNT EMILY: There's only the one. She only got the one.

VICTORIA: It's a large one, all of us can—

AUNT EMILY: Large? It is certainly not large, it's a good sized melon, but you couldn't say it was any too big.

VICTORIA: I would have bought a bigger one, Glen, I would have, only—

GLEN: You mean to tell me they had them bigger?

VICTORIA: Yes.

(VICTORIA *starts to cry.* AUNT EMILY *tries to keep* GLEN *from seeing.*)

AUNT EMILY: Now Glen, it's really quite a fine melon and I'm sure that you've got better things to do than listen to women talking about cantaloupe.

GLEN: (*Pushing* AUNT EMILY *aside*) Then why didn't you get a bigger one?

VICTORIA: I reached out my hand—

AUNT EMILY: (*Shielding* VICTORIA) Shoo, shoo, Glen, let us women get about our business.

GLEN: Vickie, tell me—

VICTORIA: (*On the verge of a complete breakdown*) I reached out my hand to touch that bigger cantaloupe, to select, to touch and smell and shake and tell—

AUNT EMILY: (*Cutting* VICTORIA *off so* GLEN *doesn't hear*) There's not enough to go around and anyway it's not what I want, what I have a taste for. Macaroni and cheese, pumpkin pie, varieties of Danish. That's what I want. That's what I want and I don't know why I don't eat it. My mother was fat and so I thought all mothers were fat, had to be fat, that's the way mothers were, fat. But anyone could see I wasn't that.

(VICTORIA *sobs quietly, gradually composing herself.*)

GLEN: Wasn't what?

AUNT EMILY: Wasn't fat. Like mother Parker. Lord, Lord, did she eat the cantaloupe. Well, if I were fat it would be because I decided to be fat, not because I wanted to be thin.

GLEN: It wouldn't be such a good decision, Aunt Emily.

AUNT EMILY: I'm thinking, maybe I've missed something. (*She returns to her washing machine.*)

AMALIA: It could happen to me right now, you know. Your body doesn't warn you when it decides to take itself into its own hands. When it consumes itself in a flame of its own making.

ROB: Suicide for the indecisive? Wishy-washy— WOOSH!

AMALIA: It is the exact opposite of suicide. It is as far as you can get from suicide and still be dead. Why, murder and suicide are practically the same thing, compared to spontaneous combustion.

ROB: You can't name me one person it ever happened to.

AMALIA: The possibility runs in the family. There have been some very close calls. My grandmother Amalia Parker was one. She was ninty-five years old when she died of old age, which is as close to dying of nothing as you usually get. Of course, old age is the body turning on itself little by little, consuming itself by degrees. But that's not a war or a car or a fall from a high place, or any other person. None of the Parker women have died that way. We've all of us died from what is inside us. Or isn't.

ROB: If one of these sex-crazed Siamese Twins spontaneously combusted, would the other one burn up too?

AMALIA: You haven't heard a word I've said.

GLEN: (*Standing up from table*) Today is the day I'm going to ask Molly to go out on the course with me.

ROB: All you've been telling me about is that one of
the genetic traits you've inherited is dying. In fact,
every woman in your family who isn't alive has died.
I believe the laws of probability will probably back you
up on that one.

AMALIA: But spontaneous combustion is one of those
times when possibility is complete without probability.

ROB: What????

AMALIA: The odds are in the neighborhood of a billion
to one, but who cares how many times it doesn't
happen, if it's possible for it to happen at all. The book
says—

ROB: The book says—you read this in some gender
specific magazine, didn't you? Didn't you? My life
is being destroyed by *Cosmopolitan, Redbook,* the
Ladies Home J. Now if you're looking to find out
about spontaneous combustion from a magazine—
Playboy. Penthouse. Hustler—now they're about the old
spontaneous—

AMALIA: The magazine only confirmed what I felt.
Identified it. Defined how I felt the heat inside me.

(GLEN *stands outside* AMALIA'*s bedroom door, about to
knock. Instead, he listens.*)

ROB: Thirty years early for hot flashes, sweetheart.

(AMALIA *dumps a drawer full of sweaters on* ROB'*s head.*)

ROB: But when you do get them, when you do start
burning up for real—well, it will feel real, so they say—
that's when I'll be so understanding. Here's the way it
works: You marry me now—and you get delivery on
belief in internal flames later. Sort of the layaway plan.
Amalia Parker Leyland. Nice ring, don't you think?

GLEN: (*Shocked, upset. He barely whispers.*) Amalia
Parker Leyland.

ROB: And the monogram on the towels—with the initial of the last name in the middle—A-L-P.

GLEN: (*Muttering to himself as he returns to the porch*) A-L-P.

ROB: Like the mountains, get it?

AMALIA: Like a molehill. I'm not going to marry you, Rob. Not with this thing inside me.

GLEN: Well, we knew it would happen someday. We knew it would happen, it happened to Mary Catherine, didn't it, been five years since we swept up all that rice and ate the leftover wedding cake and could be sure. We could be sure that it was happening to us. That it had happened.

AMALIA: I'm afraid.

ROB: Afraid? Afraid of spontaneous combustion? If I were you I'd be more concerned about the tragedy of immaculate conception. A terrible burden for a young virgin to have to carry around. But what I'm suggesting we do is the time honored cure.

(ROB *tries to pull her down with him.* AMALIA *throws clothing at him.*)

AMALIA: What are you talking about?

ROB: Your virginity.

AMALIA: My what?

ROB: Your virginity. You are a virgin, aren't you?

AMALIA: What made you think I was a virgin?

ROB: You're not?

AMALIA: Not for years.

ROB: Years?

AMALIA: What made you think—

ROB: Every single night for the past—

AMALIA: Oh, that. What does that have to do with it?

ROB: What do you mean?

AMALIA: And so that's supposed to mean I'm a virgin?

ROB: Well why else wouldn't you?

AMALIA: You're not one are you?

ROB: What?

AMALIA: A virgin?

ROB: What would make you think—

AMALIA: Well it's just that you wanted to so bad.

ROB: What?

AMALIA: If you can assume I won't because I am one, why can't I assume you are one because you will?

ROB: That's ridiculous—

AMALIA: Yes.

ROB: Amalia, why—why, if you did before, why won't you with me.

AMALIA: I'm trying to tell you why not.

ROB: No you're not. Me, you're telling me about spontaneous combustion. That's what you're telling me. If you did before—

AMALIA: I was younger then, that's all, and things seemed less important—more important...I didn't love them, the ones I...okay?

ROB: Okay? How can that be the end of that sentence? Okay? How can that word—

AMALIA: I didn't love them. But...

ROB: Then do I assume correctly, that if you, ah, "did" with them because you didn't love them, then you don't with me because you—

AMALIA: (Softly) Yes.

ROB: You remind me of the city of Saint Louis, which has more stop signs per capita than any other place in America. Each alderman in the city is allotted a certain number of stop signs, but they have to use all of them, and since stop sign allotment is a sign of prestige, and they have run out of intersections that are not already stopped, they literally build new intersections in order to use them. Their stop signs.

GLEN: (*Monitoring the weather, pleased*) A day so completely magnificent I wouldn't believe it myself if I didn't have the facts right here to back me up. Perfect. Clean. And fair. (*He returns to the kitchen.*)

VICTORIA: Did you ask Molly about golfing yet?

GLEN: Can't, Vickie. There's a big storm front moving in. (*Pause*) A-L-P.

VICTORIA: What?

GLEN: Don't these things traditionally happen at night? Of course, I'm happy to see it happen during the day, it's much safer in daylight. So much easier to make mistakes, in the dark.

VICTORIA: What mistakes, Glen, I don't—

GLEN: There's something I've got to tell you. (*He puts his arm around her.*) There is a large pile of clothing on the floor in Molly's room.

VICTORIA: Yes?

GLEN: She's leaving us.

VICTORIA: She's just rearranging her closet. She's decided to unfold some things and hang them in her closet, and fold some other things and put them away.

GLEN: No. She's packing.

VICTORIA: She's lining the drawers of the chest with patterned paper and hanging her dresses in treated plastic bags.

GLEN: It's too large a pile for that, Vickie, it's—

VICTORIA: She will slip bars of scented soap into the pockets of her suit jackets. To keep away the moths. Her clothes will smell like lavender. And if she finds a button missing off a shirt, she'll put it on a pile. And if she finds a dress that needs hemming, she put it on a pile, maybe the same pile. And there will be clothes with stains and spots...we won't be able to get all of them out, you know. But we'll try. Because she will come in here. Yes, she will come in here, when she's ready, and she will ask me to come with her, and the two of us, together, we will go to her room and I will help her decide what will be lengthened and sewed and cleaned and given away.

GLEN: No.

VICTORIA: She will come in here.

GLEN: No.

VICTORIA: When she's ready.

GLEN: She's leaving. She's getting married. (*Pause*) Does she have enough warm clothing?

VICTORIA: We don't know where she's going. They might be headed south.

GLEN: Won't need warm clothing, if they're headed south.

VICTORIA: No, she won't.

GLEN: And what about shoes? I didn't see any shoes on the pile. Does she have a decent pair of shoes? Aunt Emily once read me a fairy tale, it was about a little princess and she had to wear out three pairs of stone shoes, wear down three granite walking sticks, and suck three loaves of marble bread down to pebbles in order to find a husband. Some kind of evil spell she had to break. And she walked around the world three times searching for him, all the way around, well, they didn't have around when this fairy tale was written, it was mostly back and forth, but she did it. Think how hard it would be to wear out three pairs of stone shoes. Especially for Molly. All those caps and matching dresses and her little pairs of shoes, could fit both of em in your hand, all those things we gave away good as new, she never soiled a one of them, never ran them down or scuffed the heels or—

VICTORIA: (*Starting to cry*) No!

GLEN: I was just pointing out that it's a good thing Molly doesn't have to wear anything out searching for a husband.

ROB: These others—all these others...however many there were, it doesn't matter to me, naturally, how many there were of them that you did not love, well, what did they look like? Were they, for instance, my height? Shorter?

AMALIA: Some.

ROB: They were taller?

AMALIA: They were shorter and taller.

ROB: How can they have been shorter and taller at the same time?

AMALIA: Not at the same time. One at a time. Some shorter, some taller.

ROB: Oh. And their hair, how did they wear their hair—

AMALIA: On their heads. Rob, what does this have to do—

ROB: Did they wear it like I wear mine?

AMALIA: Some, but—

ROB: And you weren't afraid of them?

AMALIA: I am not afraid of the way you wear your hair, Rob.

ROB: I didn't think you were. Let's face facts, Amalia. If you're not afraid of me because of the way I look, it follows that you do not love me for the way I look. That's assuming a cause and effect relationship between love, fear, and spontaneous combustion.

AMALIA: Why would you want me to love you for you looks?

ROB: Because there's a certain beauty about being loved for your looks. A certain—certainty. If someone loves you for your looks, chances are they are not going to change their mind. How could they change their mind about your looks? You look the way you look. They either love you for it or they don't. And your looks are something you can be sure of, because—there they are, self evident fact, anybody can see them, you can see them too. The further beauty of this system is that if you loved me for my looks but there was this one particular part, or two parts, even, of my looks you didn't love—say these were the parts that frightened you—I could, without too much trouble, change them. If you loved me for my looks I'd be crazy not to. But if you don't love me for my looks I don't know where to start.

There is limit, a range, a—certainty—to the sound of my voice, in the color of my eyes. If you loved me for that particular sound, that shade of color—I'd be safe, secure. But there's no telling what the rest of me—if it's the rest of me you love—can do.

If it's something inside me—something I can never see and can never know, how will I identify it? How will I ever be able to make it go away?

And if what has got you frightened is also what you love—then why should I?

(ROB *tries to take* AMALIA *in his arms.*)

AMALIA: Stop it! You don't know what you're doing!

ROB: Of course I know what I'm doing.

AMALIA: (*Struggling to get away from him*) There is something inside me. Something like a match.

ROB: Your insides are nothing like a match.

AMALIA: Like a match in that split instant when someone is about to strike it. Only, it strikes itself. Rob, get back, it isn't safe!

ROB: Then spontaneous combustion can only happen if the match strikes itself?

AMALIA: Rob, look out—Rob, don't—don't—

ROB: Amalia, that match doesn't stand a chance. Not with me here. Not with old—

(AMALIA *knees* ROB *in the groin.*)

ROB: Oh my God—oh, my God...oh, my...

AMALIA: I didn't do it that hard.

(ROB *continues moaning.*)

AMALIA: It's just a myth. Just a myth. Well, no woman has ever believed that it hurts that much and neither do I. (*She reaches out to touch him.*) Let me see. Rob, let me see. Are you all right or aren't you?

ROB: I don't know.

AMALIA: What do you mean you don't know? How can you not know?

ROB: I mean they can't test parachutes on the ground, Amalia, that's what I mean.

AMALIA: Why do you want me to think that I've hurt you?

ROB: Amalia, you *have* hurt me.

AUNT EMILY: (*She drags a bulky, bright red bedspread out of the dryer and heads for* AMALIA'*s room. She arrives engulfed in the bedspread, and trips into the room, unable to see a thing. Her face completely covered, she turns toward the pile of clothing, and her body goes stiff beneath the spread.*) Molly...my God Molly...what has come over your room? (*Now she pulls the spread down so that it is no longer covering her face.*) Once I saw the way Gloria Henderson's one room with cooking privileges looked. My mother let me take the Christmas basket to her. I was very young couldn't help seeing it. (*Whispers*) It was nine o'clock in the morning and her clothes...they looked just like this. Just like this. Well I ran home and asked my mother. What it was in a woman that could make her keep her room like this? It was what she had for breakfast. (*Imitates her mother*) Every morning...a double. Every morning— (*She drops part of the bedspread to indicate an enormous glass.*) —a glass like this. Every morning— (*She looks around the room with renewed horror and clutches the bedspread.*) Here, Molly, help me, it's swallowing me up!

(AMALIA *goes to her and takes an end of the spread, but is looking for the label rather than helping.*)

AMALIA: (*Finding the label*) One of those blends.

AUNT EMILY: What? ...What?... (*She works her way out of the spread.*)

AMALIA: I cannot sleep with that on my bed.

AUNT EMILY: You can't?

AMALIA: No.

AUNT EMILY: Bright red, I've always felt, was a very common color, but it shows up some things and hides others, you understand, and on a young girl's bed, I've always felt, red was just the—

AMALIA: No, that's not—

AUNT EMILY: It isn't the color, is it? It's the masculinity of the spread, the way it looks too much like a bedspread bought, if you had a brother, for you brother—

AMALIA: *No! It's because of spontaneous combustion!*

AUNT EMILY: (*Sits down on the bed, confused and disoriented, whispering loudly to herself.*) I can't see what's wrong with it, there's nothing wrong that I can see...

AMALIA: (*Gives in*) Of course you're right, here, there isn't a thing wrong with this spread, give it to me, I'll take care of it.

(AMALIA *takes it, holding it gingerly.* AUNT EMILY *is breathing with difficulty, she's exhausted, but this doesn't stop her from bending down and picking up a shirt off the pile. She folds it neatly.* AMALIA *hides the bedspread under the other end of the pile.*)

(*As* AUNT EMILY *grabs for a shirt to fold and grabs* ROB's *leg instead. She does not see* ROB.)

ROB: And a very good morning to you, Miss Parker.

AMALIA: Aunt Emily—lookout—those clothes aren't safe!

ROB: Look at me sitting in Amalia's clothing, her most personal, intimate, most intimate and personal—

AMALIA: Aunt Emily! I'm looking for my blue dress, but I think it's in the wash—

(AMALIA *tries to get* AUNT EMILY *out of the room.* ROB *grabs her leg.*)

ROB: Maybe you didn't get a good look at me, Miss Parker—

AMALIA: (*To* ROB) Stop it!

AUNT EMILY: I've got so I can hear the wash from every room in the house. You don't have to tear your room apart hunting your blue dress any longer. Your blue dress is in— (*She concentrates.*) —is in the rinse cycle. (*She hurries to the washing machine.*)

AMALIA: You know it isn't safe for her to be so close to all this flammable clothing. What if something happened, you'd be responsible.

ROB: She saw me, she felt me, she heard me. She probably smelled me too. That's the five senses—no, only four, but isn't that enough? Four senses are enough. You know, I really make an effort. Like at meals, making my table manners just like hers, that ridiculous business with the bread and butter, those damn crescent rolls—

AMALIA: You know she won't talk to you when you're in my bedroom.

ROB: That's a room with a bed, your bed. That's why she wouldn't see me, I suppose? I'll have to ask her if I fade in and out of focus in the living room...the couch folds out to a hide-a-bed.

AMALIA: It's the way she is, the way her mother was, the way—

ROB: The way you are, is what. With your own personalized variation. You see the bed and you see me and you can see me, even, on the bed but you cannot see you with me on the bed. Even a marriage bed. Now that's the bed Aunt Emily would be happy to see and see me on and see you with me. (*Softly*) Marry me, Amalia.

AUNT EMILY: (*Approaching* GLEN *and* VICTORIA) I must talk to you about Molly.

VICTORIA: Then you've seen?

AUNT EMILY: She has thrown her clothes all over the floor. I have seen clothes like that before, yes, and I know what it means.

VICTORIA: Then you know.

AUNT EMILY: I've always known. Impatience. Close enough to a bad habit to be the real thing. Can't wait for the time of one cycle, has to have her blue dress right now.

GLEN: Aunt Emily, it's not what you think.

AUNT EMILY: It's not? Well, I know what I see. Not that I want to see it. We never want to see bad things like that in those we love but there it is. There it is.

(AUNT EMILY *returns to her washing machine.* GLEN *follows her.*)

GLEN: Aunt Emily, you remember the problem Mary Catherine had telling you she was getting married?

AUNT EMILY: The problem in these marriages is they want to be happy all the time. They want to be happy when they wake up in the morning and they want to be happy at noon. They want to be happy when they go to bed at night. Oh, it's disgusting.

GLEN: Yes, of course it is, but Amalia and Rob—

AUNT EMILY: Who's Rob?

ROB: Marry me, Amalia. Why should Aunt Emily be the only one who sees that particular, that white linen and lace, that legal, lawful wedded married bed every time she tries so hard not to see me? Marry me.

(AMALIA *shakes her head, no.*)

AUNT EMILY: Is Rob the one who eats his roll and butter with a fork?

GLEN: What? Eats his bread and butter with a knife and fork?

VICTORIA: But you're the only one who eats—

AUNT EMILY: I can see that Rob is a very well brought up young man, if perhaps a bit too delicate in his eating habits.

GLEN: Well, Rob is in Molly's room right now, and he's asked— (*He realizes what he's said.*)

AUNT EMILY: I didn't quite catch that. Where is he now?

GLEN: He's...he's...

VICTORIA: Helping Molly pack. In her room. Her bedroom.

GLEN: Vickie—don't—

VICTORIA: Robert Leyland is in—

AUNT EMILY: Naturally there is no Robert Leyland in Amalia's bedroom. I was just there. He is such a polite boy. And so prompt for dinner, I've noticed.

VICTORIA: He's on time for dinner because he never leaves after lunch. Or breakfast either, which he is also never late for because he never comes out of Molly's room except for meals.

AUNT EMILY: *Victoria, really!!! (Controlling herself)* Perhaps the young man is supposed to be here now for breakfast, but isn't yet. Perhaps even though he is polite, he is also late. Perhaps— (*Horrified*) Coming over for breakfast and they aren't even engaged! It's a disgrace! (*She dashes off to finish the laundry.*) The state of Molly's room—her dresses, her slacks, her pretty shirts. Her dresses, her slacks, her pretty shirts. Wrinkled, wadded, into little balls, stepped on.

VICTORIA: I don't care what you say, Glen. It's always worried me and it's getting worse. A person can't pick and choose what they see by what they want to see.

GLEN: She doesn't pick and choose. All this time and you still won't believe me. She cannot see Rob when he is in Amalia's bedroom.

VICTORIA: It's just stubbornness or senility and I don't know which one's worse.

AUNT EMILY: Her sweaters, her scarves, her bathing suits. Her sweaters, her scarves...

(*As* GLEN *heads for the back porch*)

VICTORIA: Glen, when are you going to tell Aunt Emily? Glen? Glen?

AUNT EMILY: (*Muttering faster*) Winter and summer, piled up in heaps, just left there, left there to lie.

GLEN: (*Looking up at the sky*) What a perfect day for golf. What a perfect day. A day when there is no possible connection between the shaft of your golf club and a lightening rod.

VICTORIA: (*Looking out her kitchen window*) It looks so lovely out there from here. Of course, I know that's no way to tell about the weather.

GLEN: The kind of day I might have taken Molly golfing. I would have risked it. I have always wanted to take Amalia golfing.

VICTORIA: It looks exactly like the kind of day when he would come home from the course. I remember cooking special for that. Whole meals that could stand and cook for an hour, two hours, three or four extra hours, meals that could compensate in the event of crowds on the course.

GLEN: I meant to someday, take her golfing. But right after she was born, the crowds—they stopped bowling or drinking or poker playing, they stopped doing whatever it was they had done before and they all started golfing. And then, the weather. It wasn't the same. It wasn't reliable.

VICTORIA: And the same exact meal had to be ready on a moment's notice if the weather blew up and turned bad and he came home early.

AUNT EMILY: (*Softly, growing horror*) Her slips...her panties...her brassieres...

GLEN: Well, the clusters of people, the mobs of them and the weather together...who could insure that Amalia and I would be able to get in even one safe round? That's when I got into the weather business. I was called, so to speak. (*He takes off his robe and basks in the sunshine.*) Clear and clean. A day like it used to be.

VICTORIA: I remember—I remember. I remember him coming home. (*Pause*) Glen—Glen—what about it?

GLEN: About what?

VICTORIA: The weather and Aunt Emily.

GLEN: Too soon to tell either one.

VICTORIA: It doesn't look too soon to tell to me. And don't you think it's time you took Robert and walked him over the course, found out now if it were the place for your new son-in-law?

AUNT EMILY: (*Growing steadily more horrified*) Her slips, her panties, her brassieres. Her slips, her panties, her brassieres. In plain sight. For anyone to see.

GLEN: (*Entering kitchen, trying to look cold.*) It's too cold out. I'll take him on an interior tour, show him the ninth, upstairs.

VICTORIA: The ninth? But you made such a point of showing Sam the eighteenth—you said it was your favorite hole, you—

GLEN: The 18th? My favorite?

VICTORIA: You swore to me it was.

GLEN: (*Teasing her. He takes her in his arms.*) And so
it is. And you know why? Of course you do. It's the
view. The view of you, standing as I take my stance,
cooking as I address the ball, the sight of you, cooking,
standing right here at the stove. (*He kisses her, then goes
to the sporting goods closet upstairs. He removes a bag of
clubs from the closet and takes off his pajamas, revealing golf
shirt and shorts underneath. He puts on a pair of cleated golf
shoes.*)

(VICTORIA *punches down the bread dough.*)

(AUNT EMILY *has taken the clothes out of the washing
machine and put them into the dryer, all in a very great
hurry.*)

AUNT EMILY: (*Louder, closer to hysteria*) Her slips, her
panties, her brassieres in plain sight, in plain view. (*She
runs toward* AMALIA's *room, screaming.*) For anyone to
see! For anyone to see! Molly I'm coming!

(AMALIA *moves to the doorway to block* AUNT EMILY *as*
ROB *takes off his pants and folds them neatly.*)

GLEN: (*Upstairs, taking his first shot*) Fore!!

AUNT EMILY: I'm coming. Molly!

(AUNT EMILY *pushes* AMALIA *aside and heads for the pile of
clothes.*)

AMALIA: You can't touch those!

AUNT EMILY: I am folding them, Amalia Parker. So you
see I can't help touching them.

AMALIA: But they're not safe.

ROB: (*Tries to hand his pants to* AUNT EMILY) I hope this
is folded properly. I never really learned, you see. But
perhaps you could give me a few pointers, "do"s and
"don't"s—

AMALIA: (*Trying to keep* AUNT EMILY *from seeing* ROB)
Oh my God Rob how could you—

ROB: You being a pro and all—

AMALIA: *Rob!!!*

(AMALIA *grabs the pants from* ROB.)

AUNT EMILY: Did you say something to me, Molly?

(AUNT EMILY *inadvertently takes* ROB's *pants from*
AMALIA, *then drops them quickly.*)

AMALIA: My blue dress, is it ready yet?

AUNT EMILY: Your blue dress? It's in the dryer, should
be... (*She concentrates.*) ...still damp, but not wringing...
wet...the front and the back of the skirt are dry, but not
the hem, not the collar, not the facing under the arms
or the pockets. The pockets are still wet, yes, they're
always the last to dry. You can over dry a dress waiting
for the pockets to dry.

(ROB *tries to force* AUNT EMILY *to take his pants. He
thrusts them into her hand and tries to close her fingers over
them.*)

AUNT EMILY: I think I'll make sure it isn't over drying.

(AUNT EMILY *runs out of the room, almost running into*
GLEN, *who's golfing. She does not seem to see him.*)

AMALIA: (*Throws the clothing* AUNT EMILY *has folded at*
ROB) You—

ROB: A shirt, she loves me. A pullover, she loves me
not. A dress, she loves me. A blouse she loves me not.
A...

(ROB *has run out of clothes and waits for* AMALIA *to throw
the next handful.*)

AMALIA: If I didn't love you I wouldn't care that you
were sitting on a funeral pyre. Get off.

ROB: If you loved me you'd climb on board. You'd be my favorite wife, my hunting dog, the horse I rode into battle.

(AMALIA *throws a huge handful of clothing at him.*)

ROB: A dress, two dresses, a jacket, a scarf. If you loved me you wouldn't be adding fuel to the fire.

AMALIA: You've been warned. If anything happens, it won't be my fault.

(*Golfing past the washer-dryer, where* AUNT EMILY *anxiously awaits the blue dress.*)

GLEN: *Fore!*

(GLEN *swings right next to her,* AUNT EMILY *doesn't flinch.*)

GLEN: *Fore!* (*He screams in her ear.*)

VICTORIA: (*Putting the loaf of bread in the oven.*) Glen used to say that he could smell my homemade bread baking from the course, and that's why he came home so early. That's nonsense, of course.

GLEN: *Fore!* (*He moves into the kitchen. He chips into the sink. He raises his club in the air in victory.*) Way under par!

(GLEN *sweeps* VICTORIA *up in his arms.*)

VICTORIA: Did you look in on Molly on the 14th?

GLEN: Aunt Emily was helping her pack.

VICTORIA: She asked Aunt Emily to help her pack?

GLEN: Aunt Emily doesn't know she's packing.

VICTORIA: But Glen, you promised you'd tell her...oh, just tell Molly breakfast soon. Tell her...all her...all her favorite foods.

GLEN: (*Golfing down the hall.*) *Fore!* (*Entering* AMALIA's *room.*) Molly. Your mother informs me breakfast is

soon. She's making all your favorite foods, for you and
Rob.

(ROB *is caught with his pants off. Embarrassed, he struggles
into them.*)

AMALIA: We're not hungry.

GLEN: Rob, you sure you're not hungry?

ROB: It's not the way it looks, Mister Parker.

GLEN: Oh?

ROB: But I can explain—

GLEN: No need to explain. I can see for myself.

ROB: You can?

GLEN: Yes. I certainly can.

AMALIA: You can? Because I've decided I want to tell
you about it.

GLEN: Molly, you don't know how happy that makes
me and your mother. Not that you have to, you know.
You don't have to explain a thing. You mother and I
understand completely.

AMALIA: You do?

GLEN: We're happy, we really are. Well, not completely
happy. These things, they tend to be more complicated.
But we understand, and, understanding, we couldn't
be happier.

AMALIA: I didn't think you'd understand—

GLEN: You don't give us credit.

AMALIA: —about spontaneous combustion.

GLEN: Spontaneous combustion?

AMALIA: I didn't think you'd even heard of it.

GLEN: Ah...well, we just didn't want to talk about it
in front of you. Of course, you're older now. Now, we

would. We'd be only too happy to talk about it, with you, now.

AMALIA: You would?

GLEN: Yes.

AMALIA: Then you aren't upset that I'm getting rid of all my clothes?

GLEN: Why would we be upset, Molly? They're your clothes. You can do what you want. You could take them, for instance, on a trip, on a trip with Rob. You and Rob wouldn't have to be going on a very long trip, would you, for you to need all these clothes, and, on the other hand, it might be...well, let's call it *the trip of a whole lifetime.* Of course, you could tell me it was going to be a very short trip, hardly any trip at all, if it would make it easier for you. We could build up to the *Big Trip.*

AMALIA: A trip? What are you talking about?

GLEN: I'd understand...

AMALIA: When you know that trips not only create friction, but would be impossible without it? Well friction is just another way of saying heat. No trips. No big trips. No little trips. No trips—not even from here— (*She points across the room.*) —to there. (*She sits down, absolutely still.*) Not even from here to there— (*Indicating a point an inch away*) —unless it's absolutely necessary.

GLEN: Then you don't want me to tell your mother you're packing for a trip?

(AMALIA *ignores* GLEN.)

GLEN: Okay, honey. Spontaneous combustion it is. Your mother and I will go along. (*He slowly returns to the kitchen.*)

ROB: This is ridiculous, Amalia.

AMALIA: Ridiculous? When I'm taking my life in my hands just by moving them? Get back.

ROB: You could at least talk to me.

AMALIA: Too dangerous. From now on, only the essentials. No extraneous movement.

ROB: Oh come on. Talk to me.

AMALIA: Only if it's absolutely essential.

VICTORIA: Did you ask her? About breakfast?

GLEN: Victoria...she doesn't want to tell us. She wants to keep it a secret.

VICTORIA: Then she shouldn't have thrown her clothes all over the floor.

GLEN: She wants us to believe it's about spontaneous combustion.

VICTORIA: Spontaneous combustion? I don't understand.

GLEN: It's her way of keeping it a secret.

VICTORIA: A secret? Does she think we can't see her clothes? Doesn't she know that I would be here, waiting in the kitchen, but that I would be choosing recipes that would not need my constant attention so that when she would ask me, I would be able to go to her room? When she needed me?

GLEN: She knows, Vickie. You know she knows.

VICTORIA: Then why hasn't she come in here and asked me? Why hasn't she come in here and told me she's leaving?

GLEN: She's afraid we won't let her go.

VICTORIA: But we will, won't we? Of course we will. (*She lights the fire under the pan of eggs.*)

ROB: (*Slyly*) Do you by any chance know how to play Fire Engine? (*Pause. No response*) Breathe once for yes, twice for no.

(AMALIA *breathes twice.*)

ROB: Well, it's very simple. The way to play Fire Engine is, when you want the fire engine, that's me, to stop, you yell red light. You got that?

(AMALIA *breathes twice.*)

ROB: Amalia, what is there so hard for you to get? If you don't want the fire engine to stop, if it isn't absolutely essential, you don't yell red light.

(ROB's *fingers tiptoe up* AMALIA's *arm. She flinches, tries to shake him off.*)

ROB: Amalia, please! Any sudden movement on your part could be fatal. (*His fingers are slowly crawling up her arm.*) You know, I could get to like this arrangement. It certainly is easy to feel the way I'm feeling about you— now that you can't move. (*His hand travels up her neck.*) Yes, I think this could work out just fine. Of course, should you feel it essential that the fire engine stop— just yell red light. (*His hand circles her chest area.*) The only thing that would ruin it for me would be if you moved. I mean, you said you weren't going to move, fine, I'll love you for not moving— (*His hand strays dangerously close to her breast.*)

AMALIA: (*Softly*) Red light.

ROB: I mean a love object is a love object is a—

AMALIA: (*Louder*) Red light.

ROB: (*Keeps going*) Unless it's really an object.

AMALIA: *Red! Light!!!*

ROB: Fire engines don't stop for red lights, Amalia, they're on their way to fight a fire.

(ROB *grabs* AMALIA's *breasts and she jumps away.*)

ROB: You make a shitty love object.

VICTORIA: (*Yelling*) Molly! Robert! Breakfast!

AMALIA: This is all a big joke to you, isn't it.

ROB: Oh yeah, sure, I'm the one who thinks it's a joke, huh? I'm asking you to marry me, you're talking about spontaneous combustion, and I'm the one who thinks it's a joke.

AMALIA: If you loved me, you'd be thinking about ways to protect me. If you loved me.

ROB: I could bring you tall, cool drinks on hot days. I could bring you tall, cool drinks on cold days. How's that. And if you loved me—

(ROB *tries to embrace* AMALIA, *she pushes him away, roughly.*)

ROB: You really don't know when to quit, do you?

AMALIA: I don't know when to quit, how about you. Marry me, marry me, like a stuck record.

ROB: Like a—consider it unstuck, Molly. Jesus—

AMALIA: I'm sorry, I—all I want is for you to say you don't think I'm crazy, you know, to be so frightened of it, that's all I want.

ROB: Yeah?

AMALIA: Yeah.

ROB: Well I don't. Think you're crazy.

AMALIA: Oh, Rob— (*She leans toward him. As she is about to kiss him*)

VICTORIA: *Molly! Robert! Breakfast!*

AMALIA: We'd better go—

ROB: Hey—no—wait—

AMALIA: You know how my mother is about breakfast, Rob.

ROB: But breakfast might not be safe, Amalia. Not safe. We don't know.

AMALIA: I eat breakfast every day, Rob.

ROB: Well that's thousands of breakfast, and who knows, this might be the one—the straw—the camel—the back—

(ROB *tries to hold* AMALIA, *she breaks away from him*.)

ROB: Oh, I get it. Your fear of spontaneous combustion conveniently disappears when you're hungry.

AMALIA: Just because I eat breakfast it doesn't follow that I'm hungry.

ROB: You know, that's the first logical thing you've said all day. And it doesn't even make sense.

(ROB *follows* AMALIA *down the hall to the kitchen. They pass* AUNT EMILY, *who races into* AMALIA's *room and frantically begins hanging and folding clothes*.)

AMALIA: (*Entering the kitchen as* VICTORIA *turns up the fire under the eggs*.) Mother!!! GET BACK!! (*She shoves her mother out of the way and sloshes water from the pot onto the flame*.) It's not safe!

VICTORIA: Well if your idea of safe is pouring water down a gas line—

(VICTORIA *takes a book of matches*. AMALIA *knocks them out of her hand*.)

AMALIA: You're just increasing the probability of spontaneous combustion.

VICTORIA: I'm not afraid of this combustion of yours. I'm ready for it.

AMALIA: Ready for it? But it would start in me—

VICTORIA: So that's why you won't ask me to come into your room? You're protecting me. Oh, Molly—

AMALIA: Spontaneous combustion is a very private thing. You aren't in any danger. You're perfectly safe.

VICTORIA: And so are you, Molly, you're safe in my kitchen, you've always been—

AMALIA: Of course, I'd damage your kitchen floor, I'd scorch it in the pattern of my feet. If it started in me right now. But nothing else—and nobody else—would be touched. You contain the fire when it contains you.

VICTORIA: (*Furious, hurt*) You're wrong. You don't know the first thing about it.

(VICTORIA *lights a match.* AMALIA *blows it out.*)

VICTORIA: I've got to light the pilot. Glen, hold her.

(GLEN *holds her.* VICTORIA *struggles to light the pilot.*)

VICTORIA: This is my stove, Amalia Parker. Now if there were some other way to hard boil eggs, you know I'd boil them that way for you. You know that, don't you? (*She turns on the gas under the eggs.*) I'd do that for you.

AMALIA: But I'm not hungry!

VICTORIA: Not hungry!

AMALIA: And what's more—*I've never been hungry for breakfast!* (*She runs out of the kitchen.*)

VICTORIA: Molly, please come back—Molly—look, I've turned it off— (*She starts to turn off the stove.*) No. She's not hungry.

AMALIA: (*Screaming as she discovers* AUNT EMILY *folding clothes in her bedroom.*) Somebody help me!

(GLEN *and* ROB *rush into the bedroom.* VICTORIA *throws the cantaloupe away, turns the fire off under the eggs, and follows.* AMALIA *is throwing clothing on the floor faster than* AUNT EMILY *can put them away.* AUNT EMILY *is in a frenzy, near total exhaustion.*)

AMALIA: Somebody stop her, she's going to get hurt!

(GLEN *and* ROB *grab* AUNT EMILY.)

AUNT EMILY: (*She has difficulty breathing*) Glen...and Rob...oh, I see, you're showing Robert about the house, how nice, you've caught me in a bit of spring cleaning here, we just throw every stitch out of the closet and on to the floor, an old custom from the old country...

(AUNT EMILY *hangs things up,* AMALIA *throws them on the floor.*)

GLEN: Fine, fine, just leave them on the floor.

AUNT EMILY: (*Aside to* GLEN) Not her private things.

GLEN: On the floor.

AUNT EMILY: They belong—

GLEN: On the floor.

AUNT EMILY: (*Begging* AMALIA) Amalia? Your father, he says...he says...he says you want your nice things on the floor. All wrinkled. All dirty.

AMALIA: I do. I want them on the floor.

AUNT EMILY: But Molly, anyone can see them on the floor—

AMALIA: I want them on the floor. Because I'm going to throw them away.

AUNT EMILY: (*Whispers*) Throw them away...

AMALIA: That way the probability of spontaneous combustion is decreased.

AUNT EMILY: Oh. Naturally. (*Pause*) Of course, in my day we didn't discuss these, uh, spontaneous combustions, not in front of men, but we always decreased the...probability... (*To* GLEN) Left on the floor indeed. You're just a man, Glen, and a man never sees things the way they should be. (*She hurries back to the washer.*)

GLEN: She didn't mean any harm, Rob. You've got to understand. There isn't a Parker woman alive who can see anything improper or out of place that she doesn't have the ability to put right. Some say this sort of mutation improves the race, acts as a protective mechanism, but we just call it "the way the Parker Women are."

ROB: The way the Parker women are?

GLEN: It's a sex-linked trait, and when a Parker woman marries, she passes it on to her daughters, and to her granddaughters through her sons. (*Confidentially, arm around* ROB) How would that feel, Rob? To be the head of a whole line of Leyland Women? It'd be known as the Leyland Selective Sight, named after you.

ROB: The Leyland Selective Sight?

AMALIA: He talked the same nonsense to Sam, too.

GLEN: Well Rob has a right to know. Just like Mary Catherine's husband Sam, he's going to be the head of whole generations.

AMALIA: Better put your money on Sam, then. I'm not carrying on anything like what I've got or like Aunt Emily's got either.

GLEN: Amalia Parker. When you know full well that Sam's unfortunate condition makes it very unlikely that—

(AMALIA *holds up a hideous, garish, brightly colored dress.*)

GLEN: Molly. Don't even think of packing that costume, it belongs to your sister.

(AMALIA *drops it on the pile and comes up with a matching cloak.*)

GLEN: And that—that goes with it, Molly, it's part of a matching outfit, you know how attached your sister is to it. Molly—

AMALIA: All right. (*She puts the dress and cloak on a separate pile, and pulls a handful of sports clothes out of the closet.*)

GLEN: Not those, Molly—you'll need those for when we play that game of golf.

AMALIA: I have never played golf before, dad. I'm sorry.

GLEN: But the round of golf, Molly. The round of golf I promised you...you could do that, couldn't you?

AMALIA: I'd get overheated.

GLEN: We could get you some asbestos sports clothes, but they'd be awful heavy to walk around in.

AMALIA: And make it even worse? Trapping the heat in, where it can't get out?

GLEN: I'm sorry, Molly, I...I was only joking... (*He shakes his head.*) Molly, this combustion thing.

AMALIA: You said you understood!

GLEN: Molly, I'm trying—

AMALIA: You are not, you are not. Not you and not mother. (*She begins to cry.*)

GLEN: Molly...baby...

(GLEN *tries to hold* AMALIA, *but she moves away.*)

AMALIA: No. You're not going to hold me and make it all right this time, I don't want you to make it all right. I want you to understand.

(GLEN *stands, with his arms out.*)

AMALIA: You said you understood.

(GLEN *leaves, stands outside the door for a moment before walking away slowly.* AMALIA *sits down on the edge of the bed and turns to* ROB, *still crying loudly.*)

AMALIA: What about you? Do you understand or don't you?

ROB: Well, I—I want to.

AMALIA: How far would you be willing to go with me?

ROB: Where?

AMALIA: With me...in all this.

ROB: I'd buy a fire extinguisher.

AMALIA: (*Disgusted*) You can go to hell!

(AMALIA *starts to stand up,* ROB *grabs her arm.*)

ROB: One for every room in the house. A custom job right next to the bed.

AMALIA: Still not enough. (*She's stopped crying.*)

ROB: I'd buy a water bed.

AMALIA: (*Smiling*) Better.

ROB: I'd purchase a yacht.

AMALIA: Better still.

ROB: To transport you to our island.

AMALIA: Almost enough. Yes, I might marry a man on an island, surrounded by water.

ROB: You might?

AMALIA: And then again, I might not.

ROB: Then how about under water? Wet suits, scuba tanks, a cozy bungalow beneath the sea?

AMALIA: (*Laughing*) You'd want to come up for air, sooner or later. And so would I.

ROB: Good. I'd rather marry you on and in this world.

AMALIA: Oh Rob, I—

ROB: Say it.

AMALIA: I can't.

ROB: You want to.

AMALIA: Rob, I do, but—if we could just find a parallel world, a world where we could breathe water instead of air, then I could say it. I'd say it. In that world, Rob, I'd say I love you.

(AMALIA *and* ROB *kiss. She tries to pull away.*)

AMALIA: I'm afraid.

ROB: Of two sticks rubbing together. But not of me.

AMALIA: No, not of you. (*He holds her.*)

ROB: I'll spend my life protecting you. One day you'll see how good I am at it.

AMALIA: Then you do believe it could happen—and you're not afraid?

ROB: Afraid? Amalia, I have never been less afraid of anything in my life.

(ROB *pulls* AMALIA *down onto the pile of clothing with him.*)

(GLEN *returns to the first level and prepares to tee off toward the stove.*)

(GLEN *takes his stance, prepares to address the ball, and looks up*—VICTORIA *is not at the stove.*)

(GLEN *hurries to the kitchen and sits at the table with* VICTORIA.)

GLEN: I'd taken my stance. My weight, it was evenly distributed. I was about to address the ball, I looked up, the way I always do.

VICTORIA: Amalia isn't hungry. How can I fix breakfast for her when she isn't hungry?

GLEN: I was ready for that last, long drive. I promised myself that shot. I had to pass up the 7th hole, Aunt Emily must be washing the green again, but I said to myself "the 18th will make up for it. The 18th, with that view of you cooking, standing over the stove. That will make up for it."

VICTORIA: I could stand there, pretending that the eggs are boiling, from the tee-off you couldn't be sure.

(VICTORIA *stands up.* GLEN *shakes his head.*)

GLEN: No. It wouldn't be the same. (*She sits back down.*)

AUNT EMILY: The blue dress Amalia's so impatient for, it will be ready in just a— (*She looks at the table.*) Victoria, your table is not set for breakfast!

VICTORIA: I'm not fixing breakfast.

AUNT EMILY: But that young man is here for breakfast.

VICTORIA: They're not hungry.

AUNT EMILY: What does that have to do with it? (*She pulls out a drawer of silverware and sets the table.*) Whether they are hungry or not, the table must be set, the table cloth spotless, the silver—my Lord, this silver is a disgrace! (*She polishes the silver.*)

VICTORIA: This is my kitchen, Aunt Emily. My kitchen. A kitchen where no one eats breakfast unless they are hungry.

AUNT EMILY: But what good are standards if you can't get anyone to help you maintain them? That's what mamma always used to say.

VICTORIA: Glen, stop her—Glen—

GLEN: You and Grandma really knew how to do it right, didn't you?

AUNT EMILY: We certainly did. Standards, appearances, we kept them all up.

GLEN: I remember the parties...

AUNT EMILY: Parties? Oh my yes. I sometimes think it was why I never married, didn't ever want the parties to stop, all the young men lined up, begging me to find room for their names on my card. Of course it was work, there's no saying it wasn't, I used to have nightmares. I would dream that all those young men had come barging into the house, but there was no food to be had anywhere, the silver not polished, and I had nothing to wear but a ratty old bathrobe, all my pretty dresses had disappeared, but there they would all be, begging to be fed, thirsty as day laborers for some punch. And I had to dance with all of them, with my hair up in braids and my robe coming open at every step. I'd finish with one only to be dragged out by another. (*She becomes self-conscious and rubs the silver harder.*) Why did they want to dance with me? I could never see it.

  I was no great beauty, after all.

GLEN: But Aunt Em couldn't make up her mind. Which one looked the best to her.

AUNT EMILY: What ever was it they saw in me?

GLEN: One might look good enough, on the verandah, in the moonlight, but come the light of day—

AUNT EMILY: (*Almost frantic*) What did they see in me? None of them could tell me.

VICTORIA: Glen, is it necessary for her to go into one of her trances in my kitchen? I don't cook in the laundry room.

GLEN: We're just lucky none of those "nasty males" looked good enough to you.

AUNT EMILY: One after the other of them did not know. Did not know what he saw in me. Imagine.

GLEN: That's what you called em. Nasty males. Right, Aunt Em?

AUNT EMILY: (*Softly*) Shut up.

GLEN: My mamma called em that too. Why I was the only non-nasty male for miles, the whole time I was growing up. Aunt Em used to—

AUNT EMILY: SHUT UP!

GLEN: (*Amazed*) What?

AUNT EMILY: I said shut up and don't you dare pretend you didn't hear me.

(ROB *and* AMALIA *have undressed and have begun to make love, their movements obscured by the masses of clothing.*)

GLEN: Wh—wh—wh—

VICTORIA: You see? There isn't a thing wrong with her hearing either.

AUNT EMILY: And you too. The both of you. (*She's crying.*) I will not put up with your nonsense, Glen Parker, do you hear me? Because I can hear you. I can hear every nasty, cruel thing you're saying about those boys, those lovely, sweet boys when I was the one who wasn't good enough, I was the one—

VICTORIA: Aunt Emily, I'm surprised at you, crying in front of Glen, you know Glen, if you cry in front of him he'll see you crying.

AUNT EMILY: *It would serve him right!* I hope he can see. I hope he can't help seeing, I hope— (*Pause*) There's something burning.

VICTORIA: There is nothing burning in my kitchen, Aunt Emily Parker, no matter how well you suddenly see and hear and smell.

AUNT EMILY: No. I'm sure of it. You've got breakfast burning in the oven—

VICTORIA: No one is hungry! How many times do I—

AUNT EMILY: Just because no one is hungry is no excuse to burn breakfast.

VICTORIA: Glen! This is the last straw.

GLEN: Calm down, Vickie, just—

VICTORIA: I have never, ever, in my entire married life ever burned any breakfast, any lunch, any dinner—

(AUNT EMILY *dashes for the oven.*)

VICTORIA: Glen, don't you let her touch my oven—

GLEN: Aunt Emily, don't!

(*A huge cloud of smoke surges from the oven, filling the kitchen.*)

AUNT EMILY: *Fire!!! Fire!!!* Oh my God, I've got to get Molly, you two save yourselves, I'll save Molly! (*She snatches the blue dress out of the dryer and runs to* AMALIA's *room.*) *Fire!!!* Amalia!!! Hurry, Molly! I've got your blue dress— (*She enters the bedroom and rushes over to the pile of clothing, waving the blue dress. She sees* AMALIA *and* ROB. *Confused, she takes a step backward to the door.*) No. I won't. I can't.

ROB: (*Trying to cover up with the red bedspread*) Oh my God—

AMALIA: She can't see us—she can't!

AUNT EMILY: I can't—but I have to—there's a fire—I have to warn Molly—I have to save her—Molly— where are you Molly— (*She tries to come closer to the pile of clothes.*) Molly, where are you, there's a fire, there's— (*She looks right at* AMALIA *and* ROB *and backs away.*) I can't—I just—maybe she's in the living room, I'll look there, and if I don't find her I'll come back— (*She turns to go.*) —no—I have to save her, what if the fire—I have to see her I have to save her— (*She forces herself to stand next to the pile of clothing. She is shaking with terror.*)

Amalia Parker. What are you doing? What are you and...you and—

AMALIA: Aunt Emily don't—*don't!*

AUNT EMILY: (*The greatest of efforts*) Fire—fire—you and—*him?* (*She points an unsteady finger at* ROB.) What are you doing! (*She lunges for* AMALIA *and tries to pull the blue dress over* AMALIA's *head.*) I know...I see!—I see— Fire! (*And drops dead, just missing* AMALIA *and* ROB *as she falls next to them on the pile of clothing.*)

AMALIA: *Aunt Emily!!!*

(*Blackout*)

END OF ACT ONE

ACT TWO

(AMALIA *is sitting in the bathtub, the water up to her neck, wearing the blue dress.* AMALIA's *older sister,* MARY CATHERINE, *has put the lid down on the toilet and sits, chain smoking.*)

(ROB *and* GLEN *sit at the kitchen table, watching* VICTORIA *arrange the hundreds of covered dishes and platters of food that sympathetic neighbors and relatives have brought over.*)

(*Floral arrangements fill the laundry area. The stove is covered with roses, and the oven is stuffed with mums.*)

GLEN: Now I admit, frankly, that I wouldn't have gone so far as to have had a fatal heart attack. Most likely we could have gotten Vickie to the hospital in time as well. But the fact that Aunt Emily did not make it...I can't see as it's your responsibility.

ROB: You don't?

GLEN: Some discretion was certainly in order. But young people make these mistakes, particularly the first time. It was your first time?

ROB: Sort of.

GLEN: Did you hear what Rob said, Victoria? Their first time.

MARY CATHERINE: Molly, when people spend days sitting in bathtubs of cold water they catch cold. Yeah, yeah, I know you're not afraid of catching cold. You're afraid of catching hot. But basically, Molly, I believe it all comes down to a fear of catching a temperature other than your own. This is why, I freely admit, your decision to silently semi-drown yourself makes no sense to me. If it is even possible to separate hot and cold, ying and yang, if it is even possible, spiritually, theoretically you still can't do it in this instance, because getting a fever is the very body to the soul of catching cold. This spontaneous combustion is just a screen, Molly. It's not what really has you scared. No. What you, Amalia Parker, are frightened of, what has you up to your neck in the wet quarter-nelson of fear is nothing more, nothing less, nothing but the common cold.

(AMALIA *ignores her.*)

MARY CATHERINE: For most women I know, a man represents a cure for a vital, everyday illness. But they can never quite remember whether the rule is feed a fever and starve a cold. It sounds obviously onomatopoeic. And the instinct once thwarted, they end up starving the wrong mouth for the greater part of their lives. They get so busy pushing men into places inside them that are not connected to even the suggestion of a digestive tract.

ROB: I mean, I'm pretty sure it was. I mean...after Aunt Emily, I...

GLEN: Don't dwell on it any longer, son. Put your mind on something else. I've been meaning to take you golfing for sometime now. (*He leads* ROB *out on the back porch.*)

MARY CATHERINE: (*Almost puts her cigarette out in the bathwater*) Well, maybe you're right. Maybe discretion is the better part of valor. If you can't say something nice, don't say anything at all, and all. You know, when we were kids I thought it said, "the better part of velour." " Discretion is the better part of velour."

Ever since then I've always suspected that discretion was somehow synthetic. Counterfeit. That's what I think now, Molly. *(Pause)* Molly, it's just not all that attractive, you're sitting there all wet, not saying anything. I mean, your little mermaid routine, I can go for that. But I keep wanting to ask you if the cat's got your tongue. Tuna fish, Molly. That's what this charade suggests to me. Tuna fish. And I don't get it.

GLEN: You bring up two girls, and if you're lucky, they bring you back two golfing partners. *(Slaps ROB on the back)* You're going to love the game. On a day like today? Naturally I can't expect Mary Catherine's husband to play, not with that leg of his. I had such high hopes for Sam, as a golfing partner, before it happened...and so soon after the wedding too. But you'll make up for it, won't you? I know you will.

MARY CATHERINE: *(Exasperated)* Look Molly I understand what you are going through, I know what it's like, but—

AMALIA: *(Screams)* You do not know what it's like. If you knew what it was like, you'd be in here with me. Don't you ever say to me that you know what it's like.

MARY CATHERINE: Bingo. *(Yells in direction of kitchen)* Hey, Ma, she's talking again.

VICTORIA: Good work, thank you dear.

AMALIA: Then—that was just a trick? Just to get me to talk? You mean you don't know what it's like?

MARY CATHERINE: How can I know what it's like when you won't tell me what it's like?

AMALIA: There's no way I can tell you what it's like unless you know what it's like.

MARY CATHERINE: Then it's just as well. People know too many things they don't understand these days. That's the way I see it. It's just a different world than it used to be. There didn't used to be so many goddamn people doing things you'd sooner die that do, all doing them around you.

VICTORIA: I have made food for other women's families. I have been so "understanding", by making homemade rolls and fried chickens and made dishes, by handing the platters to other women and whispering "I understand, dear, that you won't feel like cooking." So understanding. There has not been one time when I have not known better. *(She starts to cry, but must carry on. Inspecting the contents of the dishes)* It's not as if I wouldn't have acted on the same impulse as all these women, as if I haven't, so many times before. If this were some other woman's kitchen, this might be the noodle casserole I'd brought over. Or these rolls, I've been known to bring homemade rolls. I might have brought these rolls over here—if only this were just some other woman's kitchen. I think I saw another potato dish somewhere. *(She takes one of her own dishes from the shelf and spoons the potatoes from two different casseroles into it.)*

GLEN: *(Expansive gesture)* Look at it. You don't have to fuss over any dials and meters to know it. You just have to look up into the sky and smell the wind and you know it. You feel it. Do you feel it?

ROB: I've never golfed before.

GLEN: You can learn to feel it. On a day like today, every man in the world can. It's that kind of special day. But maybe you need some training, so if we leave now—

ROB: Now?

GLEN: If we don't get to the course right away the crowds will—

ROB: I just can't play golf. I keep thinking about Aunt Emily.

GLEN: Don't you think I keep thinking of her too, Rob? Don't you think, of the two of us, I'm bound to keep thinking about her more? Why do you think I'm asking you to play?

ROB: Sir, I'm—I'm sorry, of course I'll play with you. We'll leave right away.

GLEN: No, no, I don't want it like this, no. A man plays golf because he wants to, because it means something to him.

ROB: I said I'd play.

GLEN: Shh...nobody talks while I'm on the machine. *(He works the controls of the weather machine.)*

VICTORIA: All these plates and pans and dishes to wash and dry and return to three dozen different women. I don't know why we bother. Next week, or the one after that, it will be some other woman's turn. I'd have the lot out circulating inside of three, four months. Two or three years from now, chances are they all will be brought back here. *(She continues selecting ingredients from the dishes, shopping for what she wants.)*

GLEN: And here it is, the perfect day. Why, there hasn't been a day like today in years.

ROB: I said I'd go. I want to go.

GLEN: *(Angry)* You mean to tell me you want to leave Molly all alone in the bath while you participate in some outdoor recreation?

ROB: I only said I wanted to play because you—

GLEN: And, on the other hand, on a fine day like today...life must go on, you know.

ROB: What do you want from me?

GLEN: Me? What I'd really like?

ROB: Tell me what you want!

GLEN: What I'd really like. What I'd really like is for you to tell me what Aunt Emily's face looked like.

ROB: *(Pause)* What?

GLEN: What Aunt Emily's face looked like at the moment she saw what she couldn't see.

ROB: *(Terrified)* Her face...

GLEN: You did see, didn't you? That instant?

ROB: Her face...

GLEN: I'd ask Molly, but in the state she's in, doesn't seem fair. What I'd of given...but, second hand's better than no hand at all. So tell me. What was Aunt Emily's finest moment like?

(ROB throws open the kitchen door and tries to escape into the house. GLEN grabs his arm.)

GLEN: Rob—don't let on to the missus about the weather. You let it stay our little secret, okay?

(ROB nods and GLEN lets him go into the kitchen.)

VICTORIA: Glen send you in for the clubs?

ROB: We're not golfing.

VICTORIA: *(Sighing)* Damn weather. To think that a day like this could turn bad. So unreliable. One minute sunshine, and the next?

ROB: It's too dangerous for golf.

VICTORIA: I sometimes wish he'd just risk it, and go on out and play. But I can't say I wouldn't worry.

GLEN: *(Entering the kitchen, slapping his arms to get "warm")* Good to get inside, should have known better that to go out without a jacket.

VICTORIA: Let me put the kettle on for some hot coffee...

(VICTORIA *turns toward the flower covered stove.* GLEN *steers her to the sink.)*

VICTORIA: Woops, make that lukewarm. *(Runs tap water)* Rob tells me the weather has gone too sour for golf.

GLEN: Oh, nothing I couldn't of handled. But Rob here was worried about Amalia. Right, Rob?

ROB: Right.

VICTORIA: Of course you're worried. It's only natural. A natural instinct. Why, did you know that Glen still worries about me, and we've been married since before you were born? *(She makes instant coffee with tap water.)* You know, I think someone should talk Molly into letting a little lukewarm water into the tub. It can't possibly be dangerous and I'm worried about her in all that icy water. *(Gives coffee to* GLEN*)* I'm not saying hot water, I wouldn't say that. Just enough to take the chill off.

ROB: I think that would be a good idea.

VICTORIA: You do? Good. *(Pause while she waits for him to go and do it.)* Then go on, do it.

GLEN: Don't push him Vickie.

VICTORIA: It's pushing to ask an able bodied man to put a gallon or two of lukewarm, I'm not saying hot, it's not as if I'm saying hot, just a little bit of lukewarm water into the bathtub of the woman he loves? That's pushing?

GLEN: I'm sure he'll do whatever's necessary when the time comes. I just don't want to rush him.

VICTORIA: I have no intention of rushing the boy, I just—

ROB: Wait a minute—

VICTORIA: And I'm sure he'll do what's necessary when the time comes.

ROB: What's necessary?

GLEN: Now don't you think for one minute that Vickie and I don't have the utmost faith in you—

ROB: *What's necessary!*

VICTORIA: Glen, I know that when the time comes in the bathtub—

ROB: *(Yelling)* That's why you told me it wasn't my fault, isn't it! So I'd get her to come out. Well I won't do it. I won't!

GLEN: Is that what you think?

VICTORIA: I'm surprised at you, Rob.

ROB: *(Backing out the door)* I won't do it. I felt the heat!

GLEN: *(Dragging him back in)* I'm sure you did.

ROB: And I promised Amalia...right after it...happened ...I promised her I'd stop anyone who tried to make her get out of the water.

GLEN: And so would I, son. So would I.

ROB: You would?

GLEN: Her mother and I want what's best for her, naturally.

MARY CATHERINE: Look at it from my point of view, Molly. You come home for the funeral of your only aunt and you find your only sister taking a two day bath.

AMALIA: I always hated it when you made fun of me.

MARY CATHERINE: It must cost a fortune to keep you in soap.

AMALIA: I thought you wanted to understand.

MARY CATHERINE: Understand? I'd love to understand. You know what I'd love to understand? I'd love to understand why you are *(Yelling) sitting in this goddamn bathtub and won't get out!!!*

ROB: You don't...you don't want me to get her to come out?

GLEN: We understand.

ROB: Oh.

AMALIA: I'm afraid.

MARY CATHERINE: Afraid? Afraid of what? Come on, spit it out. Your face is getting red—come on—oooh, Big Mean Mary Cath made little sweet Molly cry? Everybody knows that people cry with their eyes, assisted by their nose. You don't cry with your face. And it's your face that's red. *(Pause)* You're ashamed, aren't you?

AMALIA: Of what?

MARY CATHERINE: You can't tell me what you're afraid of because you're ashamed of it.

AMALIA: I am not.

MARY CATHERINE: And now you're frightened to tell me you're ashamed of what's got you frightened. Compact use of emotions. Usually I admire that. Not that I'm anticipating an emotional shortage, you understand.

AMALIA: You stop making fun of me.

MARY CATHERINE: Why? It's traditional. To poke fun at those men and women who have made the decision to spend large portions of their lives in water. The two that come to mind are Noah and Christopher Columbus. Now Columbus was rewarded with his very own Federal holiday, which puts him on par with Jesus Christ, who walked over, rather, on the stuff, though I suppose that qualifies. Both old Chris and Christ did all right for them selves in the Gift from God department, but as for me—give me what Noah got.

AMALIA: What did he get?

MARY CATHERINE: You don't know what Noah got?

AMALIA: No.

MARY CATHERINE: Not what Noah—

AMALIA: No!

MARY CATHERINE: Noah got the rainbow. *(Pause)* And the rainbow, for your information, is God's promise that He will never again destroy the world by water.

AMALIA: And the next time He destroys the world... how will He destroy it?

MARY CATHERINE: Most likely, with fire.

AMALIA: Fire? *(She sinks down further into the tub.)*

MARY CATHERINE: Most likely. *(Noticing* AMALIA*)* I wouldn't worry about it if I were you.

AMALIA: You wouldn't?

MARY CATHERINE: He's broken his promises before. As a matter of fact, you could say He makes a habit of it.

AMALIA: *(Sitting up)* Yes, that's true.

MARY CATHERINE: And on the other hand, some promises, He keeps.

VICTORIA: We're not saying it's time yet, Rob, but we'd feel better if you were with her after what's happened.

ROB: I'd love to sit in there with Molly, there's nothing I'd like better in the world, but there's my mother, you see, she's sure to have missed me by now, and—

VICTORIA: You mean you didn't tell her about you and Molly?

ROB: Why would I—

VICTORIA: You mean to tell me that when you left the house to come over here, to help Molly pack, you didn't give your mother the smallest of hints? You realize, she knows anyway. With boys, it must be so easy to tell, to see when it is they are leaving to get married.

ROB: *(Frightened)* Ma-married?

VICTORIA: You were going to let your mother cook a meal and set a place for you when you knew you'd be gone? When you knew you'd be at some Justice of the Peace—

ROB: Wait a minute—that was before—

VICTORIA: With our little Molly?

GLEN: Got to ask you boss for a raise and two weeks off for some honeymoon behavior. Hell, tell him to come to the wedding and bring the whole family. That always softens 'em up. Course, we'll have to keep the guest list down, keep it a small affair. It's not what you would call a large bathroom. Adequate for our needs, though. At least, it always has been, in the past.

VICTORIA: It shouldn't be hard to find Molly something washable, in white.

GLEN: One day this week. You and Molly pick the day, the time, the number of the invited guests.

VICTORIA: I want a traditional wedding cake for Molly. I'll press ice cream into my cake pans. Under the icing, with the tiny bride and groom sitting on top, no one will know. Not that it's anything to be ashamed of. *(She rushes around the room, pointing to various covered dishes.)* The sit down dinner: The appetizer, the cold entree, the sides, the salads. Do you think your mother would like a say in the menu, Rob? I'm adaptive, within refrigerated limits. I'll give her a call.

GLEN: Your co-workers will want to set up some kind of stag affair. Give me your office number.

ROB: I don't have an office number. I don't have any co-workers. I don't have a boss. *I don't have a job!*

GLEN: *(Pleased)* Oh?

VICTORIA: *(Delighted)* Oh?

GLEN & VICTORIA: Oooooooooooooooh. *(They whisper excitedly.)*

VICTORIA: And what about your mother? Does she take an interest in what you do?

ROB: Well, in a way. She did tell me not to come back home. And not to call.

VICTORIA: *(Overjoyed at this stroke of luck)* So you haven't called?

ROB: No.

GLEN: But surely your mother would insist on knowing how you're going to spend the next thirty or forty years of your life?

ROB: Not unless I get my job back.

VICTORIA: There's no cause for you to be worrying about money, Rob. That bathroom is our wedding gift to you and Molly.

GLEN: You know, Rob, Vickie and I have no friends or family to speak of, we're pretty self-contained around here, and seeing that your situation is similar, and all the fuss and bother a big wedding always is...well, seven years go by in an instant. By the time you've turned around, there they're gone.

VICTORIA: There's something so romantic about common law marriage. The way it suggests that people in love have no idea of the amount of time they're spending together.

GLEN: In our eyes, you and Molly are already married. So why not dispense with the sanctions of church and state? Where are they when you need them anyway, that's what I say.

MARY CATHERINE: Amalia, even if the world does end by fire—that's assuming we're ruling out by ice—well, either way, fifty gallons of bath water isn't going to save you.

AMALIA: You'd be scared too. You would be. If you and Sam killed Aunt Emily the way Rob and me did.

MARY CATHERINE: Maybe.

AMALIA: You'd be in here with me. Instead of me.

MARY CATHERINE: Maybe.

AMALIA: No. You would.

(MARY CATHERINE *turns to leave.*)

AMALIA: If something inside you had killed her—

MARY CATHERINE: Stop saying that! Whatever you've got inside you, it can't be so different from what's inside me, can it? It can't. And there is nothing inside me that could kill Aunt Emily. *Nothing.* Nothing that could scare me the way you're scared.

AMALIA: Not anything.

MARY CATHERINE: Not a— (*But she hesitates.*) —chance.

AMALIA: Not anything? Not anything in you, something inside you, something, maybe, when you're with Sam—

MARY CATHERINE: What do you mean, Sam? What do you mean by asking me a question like that about Sam?

AMALIA: All I meant was, when you are with him, does he make you frightened, not of him, but frightened of—

MARY CATHERINE: Why would he?

AMALIA: He wouldn't want to, Mary Catherine, he wouldn't want to, but—

MARY CATHERINE: His leg, is that what you mean? Well his leg doesn't—

AMALIA: I am not talking about his damn leg.

MARY CATHERINE: You're not?

AMALIA: Why do you always think everybody's always talking about his leg?

MARY CATHERINE: It's just that everybody is always not talking about but really talking about his leg.

AMALIA: Well, I'm not.

MARY CATHERINE: Oh. *(Pause)* You're not?

AMALIA: No.

MARY CATHERINE: Oh. *(Pause)* You know, Molly, I'm not saying I absolutely haven't felt your kind of heat.

AMALIA: Oh, Mary Catherine, you mean—

MARY CATHERINE: I'm not saying I haven't. That's as far as I can go.

AMALIA: Oh.

MARY CATHERINE: *(Whispers)* The lame make better lovers.

AMALIA: *(Normal voice)* The lame make bet—

MARY CATHERINE: Shh. Don't say it out loud.

AMALIA: I won't.

MARY CATHERINE: Well, you can if you want.

AMALIA: I said I won't.

MARY CATHERINE: I mean, it's not as if it's some secret.

AMALIA: I said I won't.

MARY CATHERINE: Okay. *(She stands, lifts the lid of the toilet and throws away her cigarette.)* I'm hungry. *(She starts for the kitchen.)* My stomach feels like my throat's been cut.

VICTORIA: Supper's nearly ready. Mary Catherine, you'll spoil your appetite.

(MARY CATHERINE *takes a large piece of pie from the refrigerator and begins eating it over the sink.)*

VICTORIA: *(Horrified)* Oh my, Mary Catherine...darling, there are plates and forks, napkins...paper towels—

MARY CATHERINE: I'm hungry, Mom, that's all.

VICTORIA: Then you should wait for the rest of the family, so we can all eat with each other.

MARY CATHERINE: Now I eat with the sink.

VICTORIA: The sink?

MARY CATHERINE: Sink eating. It's central to the refrigerator... *(Indicates the refrigerator)* Cuts down on spillage. And no plate to wash. *(She begins stuffing the pie in her mouth.)* You see? And there's water to wash it right down. *(She cups her hand under the faucet to drink.)* Saves on the breakables, you know? And to wash up... *(She soaps and rinses her hands.)* There you have it. Sink eating. The way everybody will eat in the future. Fast. Convenient. Labor efficient. I'm not hungry anymore. *(She goes back to* AMALIA*'s room and goes through the pile of clothing.)*

(GLEN *and* ROB *enter, and find* VICTORIA *very upset.)*

GLEN: Vickie, what's the—

VICTORIA: It's Mary Cath. She...she... *(Whispers)* She must have learned it from that husband of hers.

GLEN: Mary Catherine is old enough to eat over the sink if she wants.

VICTORIA: But the whole family was going to eat together. My lovely cold buffet.

(GLEN *holds* VICTORIA *while she cries, and gestures to* ROB *to come closer.*)

GLEN: Rob, I wonder if you wouldn't do me a little favor. (*He whispers in* ROB's *ear.*)

ROB: Mister Parker, I don't—

GLEN: Call me dad. Please, do this...do it for Aunt Emily.

MARY CATHERINE: (*Holding up a frilly, delicate blouse*) Wow. Will you look at this blouse.

AMALIA: You said you'd tell me about the heat.

MARY CATHERINE: And I'm feeling it right now. (*She takes off her own blouse and struggles to fit into* AMALIA's.)

AMALIA: There's room in here for two, you can come in here with me, where it's safe.

MARY CATHERINE: Wouldn't help. There's no known cure. Sometimes I think I'll die of it.

AMALIA: (*Concerned*) Mary Catherine, what is it!

MARY CATHERINE: (*Sticks her head in the bathroom, whispers*) I like to dress up in women's clothing.

AMALIA: But Mary Catherine, you are a woman.

MARY CATHERINE: So? Being a woman, that's supposed to make it all right?

AMALIA: It's supposed to...of course it is.

MARY CATHERINE: *Ha!* It makes it easier across the shoulders, and that's about it.

(ROB *goes to the refrigerator, takes out two huge pieces of pie, and stands in position over the sink.* GLEN *prods* VICTORIA.)

GLEN: Gotta get right back on the horse that throws you, Vickie. Let's prove we can, now, come on...

(*On cue,* ROB *begins sink eating.*)

VICTORIA: *(Hesitantly, an effort at graciousness)* Rob...how does...that pie...taste to you?

GLEN: Good girl.

ROB: *(Mouth full of pie)* Fine, fine. *(He starts to turn to talk to her.)*

GLEN: No, keep eating, ignore her, eat, eat.

(ROB looks like he is about to ditch the whole thing, but he continues eating.)

VICTORIA: It's a custard pie, needs absolutely no baking. And I want you to know, that I made this pie especially for...for this kind of...for sink...eating...*(She starts to break down.)*

GLEN: Come on, you can do it!

VICTORIA: *(Crying)* I can't, I can't.

(ROB, eating as fast and loudly as is humanly possible, is about to finish all his pie. GLEN pushes VICTORIA in the direction of the refrigerator.)

GLEN: You know what to do. That-a-girl.

(VICTORIA opens the refrigerator, then becomes confused.)

GLEN: What you looking for honey?

VICTORIA: A serving piece—

GLEN: Bare hands.

VICTORIA: *(She scoops up the rest of the pie, at least half a pie's worth, and holds it out to ROB.)* Would you care... care for another piece of pie?

ROB: Uh...

(GLEN signals, yes.)

ROB: Yes please.

(VICTORIA gives him two handfuls of custard pie.)

VICTORIA: I am so glad to see that you are enjoying the pie. (*She slumps against the stove, exhausted.*)

MARY CATHERINE: I like wearing women's clothing. I like the way the fabrics feel against my skin. I like the way it pulls across here, and pillows here. I like looking at myself in the mirror. I like to imagine that I am wearing clothing different than what I have on. Well, not different. More than like itself. Skirts with higher slits. Shoes with higher heels. Bras which push up and up, very round. I like to rub silk underpants up in here, and then put them on, pulling them tighter, high between my legs.

(ROB *crams all the pie in his mouth and rinses his hands under the faucet. He makes his way to the laundry area and slides down on the floor, stuffed.*)

GLEN: (*To* VICTORIA) You did that like a real pro.

VICTORIA: It's Rob. He's such a fine young man.

GLEN: And just think. Someday they'll have children. It's even possible that...

VICTORIA: (*They have the same thought at the same moment.*) It might be a good idea to start looking for an obstetrician who delivers underwater.

GLEN: (*Gathers up* ROB *and heads for* AMALIA's *room.*) Time to face the music, son.

(GLEN *deposits* ROB *on* AMALIA's *bed.* MARY CATHERINE *is still trying on clothes, prancing around the room.*)

GLEN: I'm going to get in a few rounds, myself.

(ROB *tries to follow* GLEN. GLEN *pushes him back on the bed.*)

ROB: I'll go with you—

GLEN: Haven't had time to handicap you yet, Rob. Molly, he's all yours. (*He goes upstairs and begins golfing.*)

AMALIA: Rob, is that you? Rob, say something.

ROB: *(Watching* MARY CATHERINE *try on* AMALIA's *clothing.)* I wouldn't touch those clothes if I were you. They're not safe. *(He collapses back on the bed.)*

AMALIA: Safe? It's absolutely safe. You were right, about water, it's the perfect insulation.

*(*ROB *moans as* MARY CATHERINE *comes near him wearing* AMALIA's *clothing.)*

AMALIA: I can't hear you very well, you'll have to come in here.

ROB: *(Yelling)* Can you hear me now?

AMALIA: Yes, fine, but—

MARY CATHERINE: *(Parading in front of* ROB*)* Only thing wrong with women's clothing...no pockets. Men, wearing men's clothing, they have it made. They can give money to blind men in the street.

ROB: *(Yelling louder and moving further away)* Your father told me himself that he probably would of had a heart attack too. And so would your mother.

GLEN: *(Upstairs, golfing)* Fore!

AMALIA: There's room in here for two. Two would fit in here just fine.

ROB: Of course, they probably wouldn't have had fatal ones. Fatal heart attacks.

MARY CATHERINE: Sometimes, when I dress up like this, in front of a mirror, I remember that first time with Sam. I took off all my clothes.

AMALIA: The two of us here, surrounded by water. So safe.

MARY CATHERINE: Sam looked at me. He said, and these are his exact words, "I've seen this artist's work before."

AMALIA: Mary Catherine, please. I'm trying to talk to Rob.

MARY CATHERINE: I thought you wanted to know what kind of heat?

AMALIA: I do, but—

MARY CATHERINE: I fell in love with him and we were married.

AMALIA: *(Desperate)* Rob, couldn't you at least come in here where I could see you?

ROB: Yes, your father made a point of telling me it wasn't my fault. I mean, our fault.

MARY CATHERINE: Jesus Christ will you look at this— my old costume! *(She pulls the cloak of Queen Zingua from the pile of clothing.)*

AMALIA: Come in here with me, Rob, where you'll be safe.

ROB: I'm fine out here, just fine.

AMALIA: But if you should start feeling like you might not be fine...if you should feel something starting inside you—

MARY CATHERINE: *(She flourishes the cloak in the air.)* The Incredible Cloak of Queen Zingua!

AMALIA: If you love me you'll come in here with me. If you love me—

ROB: NO! I can't, I can't. *(He runs to the kitchen, past* VICTORIA *and* GLEN, *and sits on the back porch, shaking.)*

*(*AMALIA *begins to cry.)*

MARY CATHERINE: Molly, you're a sweetheart to have saved my old costume for me. *(She struggles into the dress, made for a twelve year old.)*

GLEN: Did you notice the way Rob came through here? I'm sure he was favoring his left side.

VICTORIA: *(In the last stages of preparing the tray)* You're imagining things. He moves perfectly fine.

GLEN: No, he was favoring his left leg. He was pulling it up short, like he had strained a muscle, or...good lord, you don't think it's his knee, do you? A man damages his knee...

VICTORIA: Rob looks like a good solid husband, Glen.

GLEN: Yes, but then, so did Sam, when he and Mary Catherine were first married.

AMALIA: Mary Catherine? Did you know that if you cry with your head lying back, the top parts of your ears fill up with water? A new, external sinus passage is created, and I feel, lying here, like I've mutated into something not quite human at all. That's what I'm really frightened of. Because I know it's true.

MARY CATHERINE: *(Enters, wearing cloak and dress, sits on the toilet, smoking a cigarette)* Oh. Is that what you're really afraid of?

AMALIA: Yes.

MARY CATHERINE: Oh. Why didn't you say so? I've felt that exactly.

AMALIA: You're sure?

MARY CATHERINE: Yes. Well, actually, in its own way it was quite different. What I felt. Which is why it was exactly the same.

AMALIA: You felt something inside you that was not like what you knew other people felt?

MARY CATHERINE: Yes.

AMALIA: What did it make you do?

MARY CATHERINE: It made me look at other women differently. I wanted to see something in them.

AMALIA: Something like what you had?

MARY CATHERINE: Yes.

AMALIA: How did you look for it?

MARY CATHERINE: In movie theatres. In beds. In...soft places.

AMALIA: Oh.

MARY CATHERINE: But I had not identified it correctly. One day I realized. That I was really, that I was truly, that I was...not...like other people.

AMALIA: Yes.

MARY CATHERINE: And I was frightened, and I was ashamed. The common combination. Frightened, that when I walked into a room, people would know. That men, would know. What I was. And what I was, was a male homosexual. I was a male homosexual who just happened to be a woman.

AMALIA: Is that possible?

MARY CATHERINE: What do you think the phrase sexual preference means? It means you prefer to have sex.

VICTORIA: There's time. For another round. Before the cold buffet.

GLEN: It's not the same. With Aunt Emily gone. And Molly square in the water hazard.

VICTORIA: You'll adapt, you'll get used to it. I won't say things will be the way they were...I won't ever be standing, cooking, over the stove—

MARY CATHERINE: *I adore men!* I love them like they were myself! Even more. At first I thought it was a simple case of confused narcissism, but then I thought...why not go all the way! I love them as much...as much as Queen Zingua. And she loved them. *(Whispers)* The lame make better lovers. *(She parades back into* AMALIA'S *bedroom.)*

GLEN: *(Joins* ROB *on the porch)* Rob? How are you feeling the weather?

ROB: Why do you tell her? Why do you tell her it's going to rain?

GLEN: Why...it is, Rob.

ROB: No it isn't. You said it yourself. It's a clear, perfect day.

GLEN: You don't know the weather—

ROB: I can tell! Anyone can tell.

GLEN: Rob, I wonder if you wouldn't mind standing up.

*(*ROB *stands.)*

GLEN: Turn around.

*(*ROB *does.)*

GLEN: Sit down. Stand up.

*(*ROB *does.)*

GLEN: You know, Rob, I've been in weather all my life.

ROB: You're lying to her about the weather.

GLEN: You can sit down now.

*(*ROB *does.* GLEN *squeezes* ROB's *knee.)*

GLEN: What's this, pulled a muscle here? Got to work it out, keep limber, a man looses the use of his knee, he might as well be dead—let's see you put some weight on it—

*(*ROB *stands and takes a few short steps.)*

GLEN: —just take it nice and easy, you know, a man's not like a horse, a horse pulls up lame, you can put them out to pasture, they do just fine. But a man, his legs, they're like his vital parts. You got to think of a man, in certain acts, almost like a tripod, can't do much good for a woman, or make much of a show on the course, one of the three is missing.

(ROB *sits.*)

GLEN: Some men, they take to golf carts. Wouldn't do you much good around the house, though.

VICTORIA: It's been years since I've set out a cold buffet. Not that I haven't been aware of the limitations of my kitchen for quite some time. It used to...confuse me. That I was able to make ordinary pots and pans and dishes too hot to place on my table, my counter, my floor. Too hot for my kitchen. But I could never make something too cold. I have never once been able to make something so cold that it could scar my formica counter, my mahogany table, my linoleum floor.

Now that my attention is no longer directed to baking and frying and boiling, perhaps I'll be able to see what can be done about it.

AMALIA: Mary Catherine, why won't he come in here with me? Why? I know he loves me—

MARY CATHERINE: Queen Zingua didn't love a man unless he was crippled or lame. Blindness was also an acceptable handicap according to some historical sources. She could have any man she wanted. A whole kingdom full.

AMALIA: Then why did she only want the ones who were lame?

MARY CATHERINE: A man like that, you can see what's wrong with him from way down the street. When he's walking toward you and when he's walking away.

AMALIA: That's why?

MARY CATHERINE: Of course that's not why. It's just easy to spot, that's all.

GLEN: I was not always afraid of golfing, Rob. I was not afraid of golfing, before I was married. Why, did you know that Molly's mother and I met on the course? We went out together every Saturday. But then Mary Catherine was born. And just like that I felt the thrust of my life forcing me to live one long life insurance commercial every time I stepped on to a tee off. Other golfers terrified me, I had to let everyone of them play through, had to keep my eye on them all, making sure I never had my back to their wood shots.

  And the lightning. Suddenly the merest possibility of a storm sent me full throttle to the club house. My irons somersaulting off the back of the cart. And all to get home safe to Victoria, to Mary Catherine, and to my Molly.

  Once I...once I...I ran my cart over the 18th green. I was so desperate to get back to them. That was the last time I ever went out on the course.

ROB: I'm sorry.

GLEN: Sorry? For me? That night, Rob, that night, I don't mind telling you, that night, together with Victoria...the image of all those golfers screaming at me and stabbing their clubs into the air, their incomplete and violent understanding of my fear as they chased me, ran me out, ran me home...that image never fades as it brings me to Victoria, again and again.

(They go back into the kitchen.)

AMALIA: Well, all the same, it must have made Sam happy.

MARY CATHERINE: What must have made Sam happy?

AMALIA: Well, I mean...you know...

MARY CATHERINE: You're not talking about his leg again, are you, because if you are—

AMALIA: I wouldn't, I would never, I just meant that, uh, when he found out about this thing inside you, this thing that has you so frightened...I just meant that he must have been very good at helping you with it.

MARY CATHERINE: Oh...well, to be honest, he didn't help at first. In fact, when we were first married, he didn't help at all. Every time I turned around, there was Sam wanting things. You cannot imagine the things I wanted from him. But I changed all that.

AMALIA: How? How did you do it?

VICTORIA: Here you are, Rob. You carry the cold cuts. *(She hands him a large platter of roast beef.)*

MARY CATHERINE: We had a...discussion. A long discussion...a very private discussion...a very private, painful discussion...one night, about Queen Zingua.

AMALIA: *(Horrified)* Mary Catherine, you didn't!

MARY CATHERINE: Didn't what?

AMALIA: Sam. You didn't—

MARY CATHERINE: Didn't what, Molly? Didn't love him? I love him.

AMALIA: But what about his leg? What about—

MARY CATHERINE: Amalia, we are talking about me. We are talking about why Sam loves me. We are talking about what I feel inside me. *(Pause)* We are not talking about Sam's leg.

VICTORIA: *(Passing several plates and dishes to* GLEN*)* I think we're all set.

(They head for the bathroom.)

VICTORIA: Molly. Cold buffet coming up.

GLEN: *(Setting the plates and dishes next to the bathtub)* Little girl's got to keep her strength up.

(ROB *tries to keep* VICTORIA *or* GLEN *between him and* AMALIA.)

AMALIA: *(Upset)* I'm not hungry.

GLEN: Got to keep her strength up, now that she's eating for two.

AMALIA: But I said I'm not eating.

VICTORIA: What your father means is, when you do eat, you will be.

AMALIA: I don't know what you're talking about. Rob, is that Rob?

GLEN: *(To* VICTORIA*)* Haven't you had a woman to woman talk with the girl?

VICTORIA: Years ago.

GLEN: Your mother says you know what happens when a man and a woman do what you and Rob did when Aunt Emily saw you.

AMALIA: Of course I know.

GLEN: Then you know what comes of it.

AMALIA: Sometimes...it's possible—a child.

GLEN: Still, possibility aside it's hit or miss the first coupla times. Took your mother and me awhile to come up with Mary Catherine here. But you're both young and healthy, and in time...

VICTORIA: *(Jabs* ROB *in the arm)* That's your cue.

(ROB *stays hidden behind her.)*

VICTORIA: Rob, it's important that you don't let this spontaneous combustion stand in the way of your natural impulses.

ROB: It might not be safe, even in water.

GLEN: Why, Vickie and me have been doing it for years, with only our bed for insulation.

ROB: But the inner heat, the two of us...I saw what it did to Aunt Emily.

GLEN: You never did answer my question about her face...

ROB: I felt the heat! Amalia, tell them how frightened you are, tell them.

AMALIA: But I'm not! Now that I'm in water, I'm not frightened anymore.

GLEN: Tell you what. We'll forget all about that question. You don't have to answer. Just one condition. *(He points at the bathtub.)*

ROB: It will just get more frightening, I know it will.

AMALIA: You weren't afraid when we were in my room.

ROB: I didn't know! I didn't know that the heat will become more intense. That the possibility of spontaneous combustion could grow! That there is a fire inside you. I can feel it, even from here. What if we let it slip out?

AMALIA: We did once.

ROB: And look what happened!

GLEN: Surely, under controlled situations, where every precaution is taken—

ROB: It's too horrible.

GLEN: *(Loosing patience)* Now see here, Robert Leyland. Are you going to get into the water with my daughter or aren't you?

ROB: No. I love her. But I won't.

GLEN: I think...I think you owe it to the Parkers. After what happened to Aunt Emily.

ROB: But you said it wasn't my fault—

AMALIA: You were the one who said he loved me.

ROB: It's already started inside you, there isn't anything any body can do about it.

AMALIA: You. You said you could.

ROB: I felt the heat! I felt the kind of heat I've never felt before in my life, Amalia.

AMALIA: That's why I want you to get in here with me, where it's safe, so I won't have to worry about you. I worry about you out there, Rob. Please—

ROB: I'm a lot safer out here than I would be in there, Amalia. Let's face facts. You felt that kind of heat before. I never did. I've been with all kinds of women and I've never, ever felt that kind of thing before.

AMALIA: But Rob, it could start in you.

ROB: Oh no, not me, it couldn't start in me—

AMALIA: Of course it could, Rob, what do you think happened to Aunt Emily—

ROB: That was you—not me—you!

AMALIA: Me? But—

ROB: That's why I've got to stay out of the bathtub. That's why—

AMALIA: You're afraid of me? You're afraid of me...

GLEN: Rob, I don't want to have to use force. (He grabs ROB's arm.)

MARY CATHERINE: You can't push a man into something like this. (She grabs ROB's other arm.) This is not the way a woman gets her man, Molly. Believe me, I know.

VICTORIA: Mary Catherine, you've got to understand. Spontaneous combustion is a very serious thing. Here, Rob, let me help you into the tub.

(VICTORIA *joins* GLEN *in dragging* ROB *closer.*)

GLEN: You're just making this more painful for all of us.

MARY CATHERINE: The way a woman does it, Molly— well, she does it alone, she does it in the privacy of her bedroom, Molly, and while I can understand that using a bathtub is an imaginative, innovative, and clean adaptation—

AMALIA: Let go of him, Mary Catherine. He's got to come in here, where it's safe.

(As ROB *is pulled back and forth between them)*

VICTORIA: Mary Catherine, now you let go of him. Rob, you must realize that no matter what Mary Catherine says, she and Sam do it all the time, and other than Sam's leg, there isn't a thing wrong with him.

MARY CATHERINE: I've warned you about talking about Sam's leg.

VICTORIA: Darling, I didn't mean anything about his leg, Mary Catherine, I—

AMALIA: If anything happens to Rob, I'll tell. Mary Catherine, I'm warning you—

MARY CATHERINE: Tell? What will you tell?

AMALIA: Let go of him.

MARY CATHERINE: What will you tell?

AMALIA: I'd get out of here and make you let go of him, but I can't, so you're forcing me, you're forcing me to tell.

MARY CATHERINE: But Molly—

AMALIA: I want him in here right now!

MARY CATHERINE: What good is throwing him in there with you, Molly, he'll just get in the way, in the way of—

AMALIA: She did it! She did it to Sam! She's the one who did it!

VICTORIA: *Amalia!*

MARY CATHERINE: Molly, how could you—

AMALIA: How could I? How could you? Sam was fine before you married him, before you married him he was just fine.

MARY CATHERINE: *(Stunned)* I'm trying to help you Molly.

AMALIA: That's why she won't let anyone talk about his leg. She did it. She crippled him!

MARY CATHERINE: *(Screaming) Stop it! Stop it!!* Don't tell them about me, don't let them know, only Sam understands about me—Sam! Sam!

AMALIA: The lame make better lovers, do they?

MARY CATHERINE: You promised you wouldn't tell! You swore you wouldn't say it out loud! *(She helps* VICTORIA *and* GLEN *shove* ROB *into the tub.) Crippled! Crippled! (She runs out of the bathroom as fast as she can, but the short, tight skirt constricts her movement. She limps badly.)* Sam! I'm coming, Sam, I'm coming. SAM!

VICTORIA: Amalia Parker. There are some things you just do not say to another person.

*(*VICTORIA *hurries after* MARY CATHERINE. MARY CATHERINE *has already left through the back door, and holds her hand out to check for rain as she hobbles off stage.)*

*(*VICTORIA *presses her face against the screen door but does not go out on the porch. She watches her daughter stumble and fall. Again, the sound of thunder)*

GLEN: Baby— *(He kisses* AMALIA *on the top of her head.)* That's it. All a father can do. You're on your own now.

(The sound of thunder, louder. GLEN *races through the house and past* VICTORIA *to the porch.)*

AMALIA: *(Timidly)* You okay?

*(*AMALIA *reaches out to touch* ROB, *he shies away.)*

ROB: Don't touch me.

AMALIA: It's all right, it's safe.

ROB: How do you know? I said, *don't touch me!*

AMALIA: But Rob—

ROB: How safe huh? You don't know for sure.

AMALIA: You were very sure before, weren't you.

ROB: Jesus Christ is that all you can talk about? So I was wrong. So I made a mistake. So I'm going to make sure it doesn't happen again.

AMALIA: If I could just touch you a little at a time. Maybe hold your hand. Just to touch you.

ROB: What is the matter with you? Your Aunt Emily is dead. We are two grown people sitting in a bathtub. And all you want to do is touch me?

AMALIA: There isn't room for two grown people to do much else.

*(*AMALIA *tries to touch* ROB *again.)*

ROB: I'm warning you Amalia—

AMALIA: But it's safe, I swear to you that it's safe—

ROB: I don't care if it's got the Good Housekeeping Seal of Approval. Don't touch me.

AMALIA: *(Hurt)* Rob!

ROB: Look. You wanted me in this goddamn bathtub, you've got me in this goddamn bathtub.

GLEN: Vickie, come on out. This is something you've got to see—

VICTORIA: I can see it from here in the kitchen just fine, Glen—

GLEN: To think I've lived to see the day!

AMALIA: This is not what you had in mind, is it? A life together?

ROB: You could say that.

GLEN: Come on, Vickie, You're going to miss the best part.

VICTORIA: But Glen, it's always been your porch, I never—

GLEN: Just this once—

(VICTORIA *steps out on the porch. A few drops of rain fall.*)

AMALIA: You don't love me anymore, do you?

ROB: I'm in this bathtub with you, aren't I?

AMALIA: Oh, yes.

ROB: And actions speak louder than words, all that crap, right?

AMALIA: That's what they say.

ROB: Then whoever they are, ask them.

AMALIA: I'd like to hear you say it.

ROB: I said it before.

AMALIA: I want to hear it now. *(Pause)* I could say it.

ROB: So? What's stopping you?

AMALIA: Don't you care if I say I love you?

ROB: You should have said it before.

AMALIA: I couldn't say it then. I can say it now.

ROB: So say it! Say it and get it over with.

AMALIA: I love you! Rob, I love you. I've always loved you. *(Pause)* You wanted me to say it before.

ROB: *(Shrugs)* I suppose I did.

AMALIA: Do you want me to say it again?

ROB: You can say it as many times as you want. You can say it till the cows come home.

AMALIA: Well I do want to say it. I love you. I love you.

GLEN: Will you look at that! The most perfect day of the century, blue sky as clear and clean as the second day of creation—and it clouds up! It rains! Rains—it pours! Thunder, lightening to beat the band. And— *we're ready for it!* A day when it couldn't rain, and it rained and *we're ready for it!* Caught everybody else in the whole damn world with their pants down, but not us. No, sir. Not in this house. No golf games ruined, no laundry on the line, no plans, no picnics... no hearts broken over the weather here. *(He puts his arm around* VICTORIA.*)* Yes, sir. I sure know how to care of my family. There isn't anybody can say Glen Parker doesn't take care of his own.

AMALIA: Don't you believe me? Rob, talk to me.

ROB: I'm wet and I'm cold.

AMALIA: I could put in some warm water—

ROB: What, are you crazy?

AMALIA: I just thought you'd be more comfortable.

ROB: Comfortable? Oh, that's rich. That's really rich. Amalia, there is no possible way for two grown people to be comfortable in this bathtub.

AMALIA: Then why don't you get out! Go on, get out! If you're so damned uncomfortable, just get the hell out!

ROB: Molly, don't cry, I'll say it, I'll say I love you, if that's what you want, I'll say I love you. I love you.

AMALIA: Do you mean it?

ROB: You know I do. You know I wouldn't be in here if I didn't.

AMALIA: And you know that I love you? You know that? *(Pause)* Well I do. Enough. I love you enough. *(She stands and pulls out the bathtub plug.)*

ROB: What are you doing, Amalia—don't!

AMALIA: I love you enough.

ROB: *(Tries to grab the plug, turns on the water.)* You don't know what you're doing !

AMALIA: Don't I?

ROB: *Somebody help me!*

(They struggle for the plug.)

ROB: Give me that plug—give me that—

(ROB almost pushes AMALIA over, and grabs her to keep her from falling.)

AMALIA: ROB!

ROB: You okay?

AMALIA: Very okay.

(They stand, embracing.)

AMALIA: You see? It didn't happen.

ROB: *(Inspecting their points of junction)* But how did you know it wouldn't happen? How did you—

AMALIA: I didn't.

ROB: Then we were just lucky, this one time, we just got lucky—

AMALIA: It's not luck, Rob. *(She kisses him.)* Does that feel like luck to you?

ROB: You mean—you mean it's safe now? You mean we're like other people now, like all the millions of other people who are not afraid of it, is that what you mean?

AMALIA: If that's what you want.

ROB: Of course it's what I want.

AMALIA: Then let me hear you say it. Go on. Tell me you're not afraid of it anymore.

ROB: I...I...I want to say it, but—

AMALIA: We can't be like other people.

ROB: But I want to.

AMALIA: No you don't. And I know why.

ROB: I know I love you.

AMALIA: Come on.

(AMALIA *leads* ROB *into the bedroom.*)

GLEN: *(As the thunder grows louder)* Vickie, the kids have got to see this! *(He goes back into the house and enters the bathroom)* Molly, Rob— *(Discovers they are gone)* Vickie! Come quick, we've got to stop them!

(AMALIA *quickly locks her bedroom door.* GLEN *pounds on it with his golf club as* VICTORIA *hurries in from the porch.*)

GLEN: Open the door this instant, young lady. You don't know what you're doing. Molly! *(To* VICTORIA, *as he listens at the door.)* I don't hear anything. Help me break down the door.

VICTORIA: They'll be all right, Glen.

ROB: Are you sure?

AMALIA: Very sure.

GLEN: *Molly! Remember what happened to Aunt Emily!!!*

AMALIA: I remember. *(She leads* ROB *over to the pile of clothing.)* And you'll remember that it can happen any time?

ROB: But it won't.

AMALIA: But you will remember?

ROB: Yes.

(They sink down onto the mound of clothing.)

GLEN: *Molly!*

VICTORIA: *(Calling off, as she tries to lead* GLEN *away)* You kids be careful now, you hear?

GLEN: Careful? How can they be careful, this is spontaneous combustion we're talking about!

VICTORIA: Yes, dear. I know.

*(*VICTORIA *gently leads* GLEN *away.)*

(Fade to blackout)

END OF PLAY

www.ingramcontent.com/pod-product-compliance
Lightning Source LLC
Chambersburg PA
CBHW052204090426
42741CB00010B/2409